GOVERNMENT ONLINE IN CANADA

GOVERNMENT ONLINE IN CANADA

PIERRE BOURQUE

Stoddart

Published in 1996 by
Stoddart Publishing Co. Limited

Distributed in Canada by
General Distribution Services Inc.
30 Lesmill Road
Toronto, Canada M3B 2T6
Tel. (416) 445-3333
Fax (416) 445-5967
email Customer.Service@ccmailgw.genpub.com

Distributed in the United States by
General Distribution Services Inc.
85 River Rock Drive, Suite 202
Buffalo, New York 14207
Toll free 1-800-805-1083
Fax (416) 445-5967
email Customer.Service@ccmailgw.genpub.com

Cataloguing in Publication Data

Bourque, Pierre, 1959–
Government online in Canada

ISBN 0-7737-5819-4

1. Government information – Canada – Computer network resources – Directories.
2. Internet (Computer network) – Directories. I. Title.

JL86.A8B68 1996 025.04 96-931208-3

Cover design: Bill Douglas @ The Bang
Author photograph: Rodolf Noël
Text design: Tannice Goddard
Computer layout: Mary Bowness

Printed and bound in Canada

Contents

V Federal Institutions

Foreword

by the Prime Minister of Canada

It has been said that the creation and growth of the Internet will change our daily lives in the same fundamental way that the invention of the printing press, the lightbulb, and the automobile did for our forebears. Sensing the personal and business opportunities presented by the Information Highway, Canadians are among the world's leaders in Net usage and development.

As shown by *Government Online in Canada*, the Government of Canada is in the express lane on the Information Highway. Our enthusiasm reflects two interrelated considerations: first, the Internet promotes democracy by allowing Canadians an easy way to register their opinions on emerging issues; second, it permits the government to make services more accessible to Canadians, and more affordable.

Our government has adopted a strategy for its use of the Internet, and has created a Primary Internet Site to provide users with a single point of access to general information about Canada and to a range of federal government services and information. The Canada Site has been visited by over one million users since it opened on December 15, 1995. This complements the use of Internet technology by individual departments.

We are also keenly aware that the Internet will not be able to assist Canadians — and especially young Canadians — to realize their full economic and social potential unless the challenge of access is met. That is why our government created SchoolNet in 1994, as a result of which every school and library in Canada will be connected to the Net by 1998. And under the Community Access component of SchoolNet, over 1,000 rural communities will be online by the same year. Moreover, in order to bring the advantages of the Information Highway to small businesses, we have instituted a program in which 2,000 computer students will connect some 50,000 small businesses to the Internet.

It is also vital for the growth of the Internet that users and potential users know what is available and where they can find it. By providing a wealth of such information, *Government Online in Canada* is rendering a valuable service to Canadians, and, I am sure, will help to keep us among the best-informed and most literate Internet users in the world.

Jean Chrétien (pm@pm.gc.ca), March 1996

Foreword

by the Premier of New Brunswick

Government exists to serve the people.

In New Brunswick we serve our people best by ensuring they have access to jobs. Without a healthy economy, our people will not thrive. Information technology is helping us build the kind of economy and the kind of society in which everyone can reach their full potential.

In the past few years the Internet has emerged as one of our most effective economic development tools. It has helped to reshape our world by eliminating geographic barriers and levelling the playing field. It has opened up opportunities for us that we could only have dreamed about ten to fifteen years ago.

Our state-of-the-art communications infrastructure has attracted dozens of call-centres, creating a rapidly expanding niche and employing thousands of New Brunswickers. Our own software development, multimedia, and training companies are flourishing. Our universities and colleges have become centres of excellence in fields as varied as geomatics and courseware authoring.

As model users of the technology developed in our province, our government has not only encouraged and supported our developers, it has more effectively served the people. With government services online, people have immediate access, twenty-four hours a day, seven days a week. To people in our cities and larger towns, it means added convenience. To those in our rural communities and regions, it means substantial savings of time, energy, and money.

Online services also make our remote areas more attractive to prospective residents and investors. Small libraries online become big libraries. Small hospitals online have access to big hospital specialists. College and university courses online transform any room with a computer into a classroom.

And we are ensuring there are more and more rooms with computers in New Brunswick by assisting interested communities to gain access to the many wonders and uses of information technology. Our Community Access Program introduces I.T. to private citizens and businesses operating in rural areas. It encourages them to integrate new technologies into their every day life, both at home and in their businesses.

In these times of restraint, information technology has also helped us streamline day-to-day tasks and reduce the cost of government. It is as simple as email, as ambitious as integrating our justice system and procedures, and as exciting as the many joint ventures we are tackling with our private-sector partners.

The bottom line is that in order to truly serve the people, governments must be online. It is more than a matter of access to service; it is a matter of access to opportunity.

Frank McKenna (premier@gov.nb.ca), March 1996

Preface

Let me be blunt. This book is about knowledge and empowerment. It is about your right and ability as a citizen to locate, navigate, and manipulate vast resources of federal, provincial, and municipal government information and services that you the taxpayer are paying for whether you know it or not, whether you like it or not.

Government Online in Canada is written in a language of focus, brevity, and simplicity. It is your key to accessing specific information from official and unofficial government sources within a huge and growing pool of related websites, newsgroups, and mailing lists. It will let you quickly locate the resources that you are looking for. It will save you time and money on the Internet.

This book will also help you have your say on the political issues of the day. It will put you in contact with key government decision makers at all levels of the political spectrum, including the prime minister, premiers, legislators, public servants, mayors, and political operatives from most political parties.

Of course, none of this would have been possible without the advent of the Internet and the astounding popularity of the World Wide Web. In fact, governments from around the world are now striving to take full advantage of this unprecedented opportunity. They are doing so because the Net is the most economical and expedient way to reach their constituents. It's as simple as that.

Government Online in Canada is also designed to help you find out about our country's history, legal system, and more. It will enable you to learn about our official symbols and the roles of Her Majesty the Queen, introduce you to the workings of Parliament and the Supreme Court, and help you keep track of your MP. This directory will also put you in direct contact with most federal ministries, departments, agencies, Crown corporations, commissions, and boards — like Agriculture Canada, the Canadian Security Intelligence Service, Elections Canada, the Passport Office, the National Archives, Statistics Canada, and the Canadian Polar Commission, to name but a few.

In most cases this directory will allow you deep access into the workings of government and will permit you to mine government services, research, and archives — on everything from aboriginal land claims, parliamentary committee reports, and bidding services for Canadian companies, to the latest exhibit at the National Gallery of Canada and job opportunities within the public service from coast to coast.

You will also find access to all provincial and territorial legislatures, and help for locating Manitoba tourism information, Newfoundland and Labrador's electronic telephone directory, arctic weather reports, Ontario Arts Council programs, P.E.I.'s nifty Island Cam, and, yes, details about Quebec's distinct society.

First Nations, too, are well represented on the Internet. This book will help you learn about the Assembly of First Nations, aboriginal education, and the inter-tribal technology network.

And what about municipal governments? Dozens and dozens have already gone online. Has yours joined the likes of Amherst, N.S., Brockville, Ont., Charlottetown, P.E.I., Fortune, Nfld., Fredericton, N.B., Gatineau, Que., Edmonton, Alta., Saskatoon, Sask., Vancouver, B.C., and Winnipeg, Man.? If not, what are they waiting for?

Governments worldwide also await your online visit. In these pages you will discover links to countries like Australia, Estonia, France, Hong Kong, Malaysia, Poland, Saudi Arabia, and the United States, plus august bodies like the United Nations, NATO, and the European Commission.

As well, this book hooks you up to most recognized political parties, educational institutions, and various public advocacy groups devoted to freedom of speech, privacy, and democracy in Canada. It also includes valuable online tools and resources for journalists and students, and unique online glossaries of terms to help you better understand terminology used in government, on the Internet, and within the computer industry. It's a novel approach that will help you remain current in an online environment of frantic change and evolution.

Government Online in Canada is not just a user-friendly government and political directory. It is also an important educational tool which will allow us, citizens of this great country, to better understand ourselves and the workings of our various levels of government. We live in a tolerant and just society, some say the greatest country on earth. Together, through better cooperation between citizens and government, Canada as a democratic nation can only grow and prosper. I truly believe that.

Pierre Bourque (pierre@achilles.net), May 1996

Acknowledgements

A few short months ago this book was but an idea and could not have morphed into reality without the thoughtful support and input of several key people.

First, I would like to express my gratitude to Prime Minister Jean Chrétien and New Brunswick Premier Frank McKenna for seeing the merit of this project and for taking the time to write down their invigorating thoughts about government's role within the expanding confines of the Internet. Both Dave McKinnis of the Prime Minister's Office and Nicole Picot in Premier McKenna's office were of great assistance with their enthusiasm and logistics.

Mike Duffy, perhaps Parliament Hill's most recognizable and best-loved journalist, came onside early on. He and I have been discussing the expanding social consequences of the Internet for a number of years now. He is surely among the most "Net-savvy" of all political journalists in Canada and I value his friendship and advice.

At Stoddart, I would like to thank Stephen Quick, a man with a keen grasp of the online information revolution. He gave me the early opportunity to develop *Government Online in Canada* and supported it with intoxicating exuberance and the greatest of latitude. I would also like to thank my editor, Kevin Linder, who helped breathe life into a rather novel directory style by sewing together a large list of websites with sensitivity and deft professionalism. It was an education and was greatly appreciated.

I would also like to thank Jim Creskey, Ross Dickson, Kate Malloy, and Rosaleen Dickson at *The Hill Times*, Canada's Parliamentary newspaper, for giving me the initial and continuing platform to explore government, new information technologies, and the Internet. All confirmed political junkies, they were among the first in Canada to gauge a tangible public interest in online government activities, and for that I am extremely grateful.

Finally, I would like to recognize the continuing work being undertaken by the people in government at all levels who have accepted the challenge and responsibility of providing highly useful content and design in the many government online offerings listed in this directory.

An Overview of Canada

Government Online in Canada

About Canada

Our country is as diverse as it is large. These sites introduce Canada and all of its many facets.

http://canada.gc.ca/canadiana/faitc/fa1.html

MAP OF CANADA
http://canada.gc.ca/canadiana/map_e.html

CANADA FACT SHEET
http://canada.gc.ca/canadiana/faitc/faind_e.html

CANADIANA — INDEX
http://canada.gc.ca/canadiana/cdaind_e.html

CAPITAL OF CANADA
(A pictorial tour)
http://www.ottawa.com/ottawa/

PROVINCES AND TERRITORIES
http://canada.gc.ca/canadiana/proind_e.html

HISTORY
http://canada.gc.ca/canadiana/faitc/fa14.html

GOVERNMENT
http://canada.gc.ca/canadiana/faitc/fa15.html

LEGAL SYSTEM
http://canada.gc.ca/canadiana/faitc/fa16.html

ECONOMY AND TRADE
http://canada.gc.ca/canadiana/faitc/fa17.html

EDUCATION
http://canada.gc.ca/canadiana/faitc/fa18.html

WOMEN
http://canada.gc.ca/canadiana/faitc/fa19.html

GEOGRAPHY
http://canada.gc.ca/canadiana/faitc/fa20.html

ENVIRONMENT
http://canada.gc.ca/canadiana/faitc/fa21.html

CLIMATE
http://canada.gc.ca/canadiana/faitc/fa22.html

AGRICULTURE
http://canada.gc.ca/canadiana/faitc/fa23.html

ENERGY
http://canada.gc.ca/canadiana/faitc/fa24.html

TRANSPORTATION
http://canada.gc.ca/canadiana/faitc/fa25.html

MULTICULTURALISM
http://canada.gc.ca/canadiana/faitc/fa26.html

INTERNATIONAL DEVELOPMENT ASSISTANCE
http://canada.gc.ca/canadiana/faitc/fa27.html

ARTS
http://canada.gc.ca/canadiana/faitc/fa28.html

SPORTS
http://canada.gc.ca/canadiana/faitc/fa29.html

ROYAL CANADIAN MOUNTED POLICE
http://canada.gc.ca/canadiana/faitc/fa30.html

FIRST NATIONS
http://canada.gc.ca/canadiana/faitc/fa31.html

INUIT
http://canada.gc.ca/canadiana/faitc/fa32.html

Canada's National Symbols

Do you know the official symbols of our country? The Government of Canada has several, including a coat of arms, the national anthem, the maple leaf, and even a beaver! Find out for yourself by visiting the following sites:

http://canada.gc.ca/canadiana/symb_e.html

ORIGIN OF THE NAME "CANADA"
http://canada.gc.ca/canadiana/orig_e.html

ARMS OF CANADA
http://canada.gc.ca/canadiana/armm_e.html

NATIONAL ANTHEM
http://canada.gc.ca/canadiana/anthm_e.html

Listen to "O Canada"
http://canada.gc.ca/canadiana/o-cda.au

CANADIAN FLAG
http://canada.gc.ca/canadiana/flag_e.html

CANADA'S NATIONAL COLOURS
(Red & white)
http://canada.gc.ca/canadiana/color_e.html

MAPLE LEAF
http://canada.gc.ca/canadiana/leaf_e.html

BEAVER
(An official emblem of Canada and a symbol of the sovereignty of Canada since March 24, 1975)
http://canada.gc.ca/canadiana/beave_e.html

The Crown

Government Online in Canada

The Queen of Canada

HER MAJESTY QUEEN ELIZABETH II
http://canada.gc.ca/howgoc/queen/quind_e.html
Click on the delightful photo of Her Majesty to see it full size.

BIOGRAPHY
http://canada.gc.ca/howgoc/queen/qubio_e.html

The Governor General

THE RIGHT HONOURABLE ROMEO LEBLANC, THE GOVERNOR GENERAL AND COMMANDER-IN-CHIEF OF CANADA
http://canada.gc.ca/howgoc/govgen/ggind_e.html

BIOGRAPHY
http://canada.gc.ca/howgoc/govgen/ggbio_e.html

ROLE AND RESPONSIBILITIES OF THE GOVERNOR GENERAL
http://canada.gc.ca/howgoc/govgen/ggfact_e.html

The Parliament of Canada

Government Online in Canada

Introduction to Parliament

GOVERNMENT OF CANADA
http://canada.gc.ca/

Table of Contents
http://canada.gc.ca/main_e.html

What's New
http://canada.gc.ca/whats/whaind_e.html

What's New Archive
http://canada.gc.ca/whats/arch96_e.html

SEND YOUR COMMENTS
http://canada.gc.ca/comments/form_e.html

GOVERNMENT OVERVIEW
http://canada.gc.ca/howgoc/howind_e.html

HOW CANADIANS GOVERN THEMSELVES,
BY SENATOR EUGENE A. FORSEY
http://canada.gc.ca/howgoc/forsey/forsey_e.html

Here you will find an important text by a remarkable man which offers an overview of our system of government and provides information about Canada's Constitution, the judicial system, and more.

PARLIAMENTARY INTERNET
http://www.parl.gc.ca/

This is Parliament Hill's online address, to find out what's new on the Hill and to retrieve visitor information. It also offers an online tour of Parliament and provides links to a number of informative parliamentary reports.

The Prime Minister's Office

http://canada.gc.ca/english/pmo/index.htm

ABOUT PRIME MINISTER JEAN CHRÉTIEN
http://canada.gc.ca/english/pmo/bio_e.htm

WHAT'S NEW
http://canada.gc.ca/english/pmo/whatsnew.htm

A MESSAGE FROM THE RT. HON. JEAN CHRÉTIEN
http://canada.gc.ca/english/pmo/pm_e.htm

FACT SHEETS
http://canada.gc.ca/english/pmo/fact_sheet/index.htm

PRESS RELEASES
http://canada.gc.ca/english/pmo/releases/index.htm

PRIME MINISTER'S SPEECHES
http://canada.gc.ca/english/pmo/pm_speech/index.htm

SEND A MESSAGE TO THE PRIME MINISTER
http://canada.gc.ca/english/pmo/e_corres.htm

The House of Commons

SPEECH FROM THE THRONE
http://www.parl.gc.ca/english/hansard/001-96-02-27/001G01E.html

PARLIAMENTARY CALENDAR
http://www.parl.gc.ca/calendar/english/calpre.htm

HANSARD
http://www.parl.gc.ca/cgi-bin/hansard/e_hansard_master.pl

MEMBERS OF PARLIAMENT
http://www.parl.gc.ca/english/members/alpha/alpha_a.htm

Liberal Party MPs
http://www.parl.gc.ca/english/members/party/liberal.htm

Bloc Québécois MPs
http://www.parl.gc.ca/english/members/party/bloc.htm

Reform Party MPs
http://www.parl.gc.ca/english/members/party/reform.htm

New Democratic Party MPs
http://www.parl.gc.ca/english/members/party/new.htm

Progressive Conservative Party MPs
http://www.parl.gc.ca/english/members/party/progress.htm

Independent Liberal
http://www.parl.gc.ca/english/members/party/indlib.htm

Independent MPs
http://www.parl.gc.ca/english/members/party/independ.htm

COMMITTEES OF THE HOUSE OF COMMONS

http://www.parl.gc.ca/cgi-bin/committees352/english_master.pl

Offers the list of Members of the Committee, transcripts, minutes, and the log.

Standing Joint Committee on the Library of Parliament
http://www.parl.gc.ca/cgi-bin/committees352/english_committee.pl?libr

Standing Joint Committee on Official Languages
http://www.parl.gc.ca/cgi-bin/committees352/english_committee.pl?olan

Standing Joint Committee on Scrutiny of Regulations
http://www.parl.gc.ca/cgi-bin/committees352/english_committee.pl?regu

Special Committee on a Code of Conduct
http://www.parl.gc.ca/cgi-bin/committees352/english_committee.pl?sjcc

Standing Committee on Aboriginal Affairs and Northern Development
http://www.parl.gc.ca/cgi-bin/committees352/english_committee.pl?iand

Standing Committee on Agriculture and Agri-Food
http://www.parl.gc.ca/cgi-bin/committees352/english_committee.pl?agfo

Standing Committee on Canadian Heritage
http://www.parl.gc.ca/cgi-bin/committees352/english_committee.pl?heri

Standing Committee on Citizenship and Immigration
http://www.parl.gc.ca/cgi-bin/committees352/english_committee.pl?cits

Standing Committee on Environment and Sustainable Development
http://www.parl.gc.ca/cgi-bin/committees352/english_committee.pl?sust

Standing Committee on Finance
http://www.parl.gc.ca/cgi-bin/committees352/english_committee.pl?fine

Standing Committee on Fisheries and Oceans
http://www.parl.gc.ca/cgi-bin/committees352/english_committee.pl?ocea

Standing Committee on Foreign Affairs and International Trade
http://www.parl.gc.ca/cgi-bin/committees352/english_committee.pl?fore

Standing Committee on Government Operations
http://www.parl.gc.ca/cgi-bin/committees352/english_committee.pl?govo

Standing Committee on Health
http://www.parl.gc.ca/cgi-bin/committees352/english_committee.pl?sant

Standing Committee on Human Resources Development
http://www.parl.gc.ca/cgi-bin/committees352/english_committee.pl?reso

Standing Committee on Human Rights and the Status of Persons with Disabilities
http://www.parl.gc.ca/cgi-bin/committees352/english_committee.pl?huso

Standing Committee on Industry
http://www.parl.gc.ca/cgi-bin/committees352/english_committee.pl?indu

Standing Committee on Justice and Legal Affairs
http://www.parl.gc.ca/cgi-bin/committees352/english_committee.pl?jula

Standing Committee on Liaison
http://www.parl.gc.ca/cgi-bin/committees352/english_committee.pl?liai

Standing Committee on National Defence and Veterans' Affairs
http://www.parl.gc.ca/cgi-bin/committees352/english_committee.pl?defa

Standing Committee on Natural Resources
http://www.parl.gc.ca/cgi-bin/committees352/english_committee.pl?natu

Standing Committee on Procedure and House Affairs
http://www.parl.gc.ca/cgi-bin/committees352/english_committee.pl?haff

Standing Committee on Public Accounts
http://www.parl.gc.ca/cgi-bin/committees352/english_committee.pl?acct

Standing Committee on Transport
http://www.parl.gc.ca/cgi-bin/committees352/english_committee.pl?port

SUBCOMMITTEES OF THE HOUSE OF COMMONS

Subcommittee on Aboriginal Education
http://www.parl.gc.ca/cgi-bin/committees352/english_committee.pl?sabe

Subcommittee on Bill C-222, An Act to Amend the Food and Drugs Act
http://www.parl.gc.ca/cgi-bin/committees352/english_committee.pl?sfda

Subcommittee on Bill C-3, An Act to Amend the Canada Labour Code (Nuclear Undertakings)
http://www.parl.gc.ca/cgi-bin/committees352/english_committee.pl?slab

Subcommittee on Environmental Awareness for Sustainability
http://www.parl.gc.ca/cgi-bin/committees352/english_committee.pl?sdef

Subcommittee on HIV/AIDS
http://www.parl.gc.ca/cgi-bin/committees352/english_committee.pl?shiv

Subcommittee on National Security
http://www.parl.gc.ca/cgi-bin/committees352/english_committee.pl?sena

Subcommittee on Private Members' Business
http://www.parl.gc.ca/cgi-bin/committees352/english_committee.pl?spra

Subcommittee on the Budget
http://www.parl.gc.ca/cgi-bin/committees352/english_committee.pl?budg

Subcommittee on the Business of Supply
http://www.parl.gc.ca/cgi-bin/committees352/english_committee.pl?sbus

The Senate

WHAT'S NEW
http://www.parl.gc.ca/english/enew.html

MEMBERS OF THE SENATE
http://www.parl.gc.ca/english/senate/bio-e/bio-e.htm

SENATE COMMITTEES
http://www.magi.com/~sencom/

Committees
http://www.parl.gc.ca/english/senate/com-e/intro1-e.htm

Mandates
http://www.magi.com/~sencom/prof.html#man

HANSARD
http://www.parl.gc.ca/english/senate/deb-e/deb-e.htm

JOURNALS
http://www.parl.gc.ca/english/senate/jour-e/jour-e.htm

SEND YOUR COMMENTS
http://www.parl.gc.ca/english/comments.html

Federal Government Programs

FEDERAL PROGRAMS — INDEX
http://canada.gc.ca/programs/pgrind_e.html

REFERENCE CANADA
(Important coast-to-coast local and toll free government phone numbers)
http://canada.gc.ca/programs/refcda/refcda_e.html

CANADA BUSINESS SERVICE CENTRES
http://info.ic.gc.ca/opengov/cbsc/english/index.html

Offers business access to information on government services, programs, and regulations. It is organized by province.

CANADIAN FOREST SERVICE
http://nrc.gc.ca/cfs/index.html

CANADIAN TOURISM COMMISSION
http://info.ic.gc.ca/Tourism/

UNEMPLOYMENT INSURANCE PROGRAM
http://island.net/%7Ecec/uip.html

General Information
http://island.net/%7Ecec/uigen.html

Types of Benefits
http://island.net/%7Ecec/uiben.html

How to Apply
http://island.net/%7Ecec/uihow.html

Rights and Obligations
http://island.net/%7Ecec/uirts.html

OPEN BIDDING SERVICE

http://www.obs.ism.ca/emenu.html

Billed as "online access to thousands of government business opportunities."

General Info

http://www.obs.ism.ca/eginfo.html

Participating Organizations

http://www.obs.ism.ca/epart.html

Current Opportunities

http://www.obs.ism.ca/etoday.html

Press Releases

http://www.obs.ism.ca/epress.html

Customer Service Hotline

http://www.obs.ism.ca/ecsr.html
Email: mthibau@fed.ism.ca

GOVERNMENT ELECTRONIC DIRECTORY SERVICES

http://canada.gc.ca/search/direct500/geds_e.html

The government's electronic telephone directory, with over 160,000 listings.

The Office of the Auditor General

OFFICE OF THE AUDITOR GENERAL
http://www.oag-bvg.gc.ca/

REPORT OF THE AUDITOR GENERAL OF CANADA
http://www.oag-bvg.gc.ca/annual/home/menu3e.html

OTHER PUBLICATIONS
http://www.oag-bvg.gc.ca/annual/home/menu2e.html

The Supreme Court of Canada

Government Online in Canada

The Supreme Court

http://www.gc.ca/sup_courtdocs/supcourt.help.html

ADMINISTRATION OF THE COURT
http://www.gc.ca/sup_courtdocs/html/administration.html

THE SUPREME COURT TODAY
http://www.gc.ca/sup_courtdocs/html/today.html

THE SUPREME COURT BUILDING
http://www.gc.ca/sup_courtdocs/html/court_building.html

CURRENT MEMBERS OF THE SUPREME COURT
http://www.gc.ca/sup_courtdocs/html/members.html

The Right Honourable Antonio Lamer, P.C.
(Chief Justice of Canada)
http://www.gc.ca/sup_courtdocs/html/justice01.html

The Honourable Mr. Justice Gerard V. La Forest
http://www.gc.ca/sup_courtdocs/html/justice02.html

The Honourable Madam Justice Claire L'Heureux-Dube
http://www.gc.ca/sup_courtdocs/html/justice03.html

The Honourable Mr. Justice John Sopinka
http://www.gc.ca/sup_courtdocs/html/justice04.html

The Honourable Mr. Justice Charles Doherty Gonthier
http://www.gc.ca/sup_courtdocs/html/justice09.html

The Honourable Mr. Justice Peter deCarteret Cory
http://www.gc.ca/sup_courtdocs/html/justice06.html

The Honourable Madam Justice Beverley McLachlin
http://www.gc.ca/sup_courtdocs/html/justice07.html

The Honourable Mr. Justice Frank Iacobucci
http://www.gc.ca/sup_courtdocs/html/justice08.html

The Honourable Mr. Justice John C. Major
http://www.gc.ca/sup_courtdocs/html/justice10.html

PAST CHIEF JUSTICES
http://www.gc.ca/sup_courtdocs/html/chief_justices.html

PAST JUSTICES
http://www.gc.ca/sup_courtdocs/html/puisne.html

REGISTRAR OF THE SUPREME COURT
http://www.gc.ca/sup_courtdocs/html/registrar.html

Federal Institutions

Government Online in Canada

Federal Government Ministries, Agencies, Crown Corporations

MAJOR FEDERAL DEPARTMENTS — INDEX
http://canada.gc.ca/depts/major/depind_e.html

Agriculture and Agri-Food Canada

http://aceis.agr.ca/newintre.html

MINISTER'S OFFICE
http://aceis.agr.ca/minoffe.html

BUDGET
http://aceis.agr.ca/budget96/ebudget.htm

TELEPHONE NUMBERS (Local, 1-800, fax)
http://aceis.agr.ca/telnume.html
and http://aceis.agr.ca/aceise.html
or download complete dept. telephone directory
http://aceis.agr.ca/contacts/contctse.html

WHAT'S NEW
http://aceis.agr.ca/newe.html

WHAT'S HOT
http://aceis.agr.ca/hote.html

TABLE OF CONTENTS
http://aceis.agr.ca/agmaine.html

AGRIWEB CANADA
(A central directory of online Canadian agriculture and agri-food information)
http://aceis.agr.ca/agriweb/agriweb.htm

LISTSERVS AND MAILING LISTS
http://aceis.agr.ca/listsrve.html

ACCESS TO OTHER DATABASES
http://aceis.agr.ca/bbse.html

Atlantic Canada Opportunities Agency

http://www.acoa.ca/

ACOA works to develop and improve the economies of Atlantic Canadian provinces.

PROGRAMS

http://www.acoa.ca/htm/programs.htm

ACOA HOTLIST

(With links to local freenets, Atlantic Canada business, education, and technology sectors)
http://www.acoa.ca/htm/links.htm

SEND YOUR COMMENTS

Email: comments@csi.nb.ca

Atlantic Pilotage Authority Canada

http://canada.gc.ca/depts/agencies/apaind_e.html

This is a Crown corporation and one of four pilotage authorities in Canada.

This site is not yet fully developed at the time of publication of this book and offers limited information pertaining to the authority's mandate and field of responsibility.

Atomic Energy Control Board

http://www.gc.ca/aecb/homepage.htm

ABOUT THE AECB
http://www.gc.ca/aecb/whatdo.htm

DOCUMENTS
http://www.gc.ca/aecb/docs.htm

LINKS TO OTHER NUCLEAR-RELATED WEB SITES
http://www.gc.ca/aecb/links.htm

NUCLEAR INDUSTRY PICTURE TOUR
http://www.gc.ca/aecb/docs/ar95/eng/pictour.htm

SEND YOUR COMMENTS
http://www.gc.ca/aecb/contact.htm

Atomic Energy of Canada Limited

http://www.aecl.ca/

Atomic Energy of Canada Limited undertakes research into nuclear energy and develops commercial applications. It is also responsible for the CANDU nuclear reactor technology. This site offers an overview of activities, a picture of a nuclear reactor, and

OVERVIEW
http://www.aecl.ca/over.htm

Synopsis of Canada's Nuclear History
http://www.aecl.ca/hist.html

AECL's website also has links to the following:

Sudbury Neutrino Observatory (SNO)
Canadian Nuclear Society
WWW Virtual Library - Nuclear Engineering
The Uranium Institute

SEND YOUR COMMENTS
Email: webmaster@crl.aecl.ca

Bank of Canada

http://www.bank-banque-canada.ca/

BOARD OF DIRECTORS
http://www.bank-banque-canada.ca/english/director.htm

GOVERNOR
http://www.bank-banque-canada.ca/english/thiessen.htm

PUBLICATIONS
http://www.bank-banque-canada.ca/english/pubs.htm

CURRENT MARKET RATES
http://www.bank-banque-canada.ca/english/fmd.htm

LIBRARY
http://ftp.bank-banque-canada.ca/library/lib.htm

CURRENCY MUSEUM
http://www.bank-banque-canada.ca/english/museum.htm

CANADA SAVINGS BONDS
http://www.bank-banque-canada.ca/csb-oec/csbae.htm

WEEKLY FINANCIAL STATISTICS
http://www.bank-banque-canada.ca/english/wfsgen.htm

BANK NOTES
http://www.bank-banque-canada.ca/english/bnote.htm

MONETARY POLICY
http://www.bank-banque-canada.ca/english/monopol.htm

CENTRAL BANKING SERVICES

http://www.bank-banque-canada.ca/english/bserv.htm

DEBT MANAGEMENT

http://www.bank-banque-canada.ca/english/debtmang.htm

Business Development Bank of Canada

http://www.bdc.ca/

ABOUT BDC
http://www.bdc.ca/htdocs/bdcinfo2.htm

BRANCHES
http://www.bdc.ca/htdocs/branche2.htm

YOUNG ENTREPRENEUR AWARDS
http://www.bdc.ca/htdocs/bdc_yea2.htm

PROFITS NEWSLETTER
http://www.bdc.ca/htdocs/profits2.htm

Canada Council

http://www.ffa.ucalgary.ca/cc/index.html

WHAT'S NEW
http://www.ffa.ucalgary.ca/cc/whatsnew.html

ABOUT CANADA COUNCIL
http://www.ffa.ucalgary.ca/cc/about.html

STRATEGIC PLAN
http://www.ffa.ucalgary.ca/cc/design-index.html

CANADIAN COMMISSION FOR UNESCO
http://www.ffa.ucalgary.ca/cc/others.html#UNESCO

PUBLIC LENDING RIGHT COMMISSION
http://www.ffa.ucalgary.ca/cc/others.html#LENDING

PROGRAMS
http://www.ffa.ucalgary.ca/cc/programs-e.html

HOW TO REACH THEM
http://www.ffa.ucalgary.ca/cc/reachus.html

LIST OF PROGRAMS AND OFFICERS
http://www.ffa.ucalgary.ca/cc/list-e.html

Canada Deposit Insurance Corporation

http://canada.gc.ca/depts/agencies/cdiind_e.html

The Canada Deposit Insurance Corporation provides limited insurance against loss on deposits in financial institutions.

This site is not yet fully developed at the time of publication of this book and offers limited information pertaining to the corporation's mandate and field of responsibility.

Canada Labour Relations Board

http://canada.gc.ca/depts/agencies/clrind_e.html

The Canada Labour Relations Board is a quasi-judicial body pertaining to the administration of part of the Canada Labour Code.

This site is not yet fully developed at the time of publication of this book and offers limited information pertaining to the board's mandate and field of responsibility.

Canada Lands Company Limited

http://www.clc.ca/clc_eng.htm

The Canada Lands Company deals with real and personal property but has no budget or employees.

This site offers limited information, including several regional telephone numbers for persons requiring further details.

Canada Mortage and Housing Corporation

http://www.cmhc-schl.gc.ca/cmhc.html

ABOUT CMHC
http://www.cmhc-schl.gc.ca/InfoCMHC/

HOW TO REACH THEM
http://www.cmhc-schl.gc.ca/InfoCMHC/contact.html

WHAT'S NEW
http://www.cmhc-schl.gc.ca/WhatsNew/

PRESS RELEASES
http://www.cmhc-schl.gc.ca/PAC/Press/

HOUSING INFORMATION CENTRE
http://www.cmhc-schl.gc.ca/Centres/CHIC/

PRODUCTS AND PUBLICATIONS
http://www.cmhc-schl.gc.ca/Centres/CHIC/chicprod.html

SERVICES
http://www.cmhc-schl.gc.ca/Centres/CHIC/chicserv.html

MARKET ANALYSIS
http://www.cmhc-schl.gc.ca/Centres/MAC/

STUDIES
http://www.cmhc-schl.gc.ca/Centres/MAC/Studies/conpref.html

PUBLICATIONS
http://www.cmhc-schl.gc.ca/Centres/MAC/Publications/

MARKET REPORTS
http://www.cmhc-schl.gc.ca/Centres/MAC/Reports/

CONTACTS
http://www.cmhc-schl.gc.ca/Centres/MAC/listings.html

MORTGAGE INSURANCE
http://www.cmhc-schl.gc.ca/Products/MortIns/

CANADIAN CENTRE FOR PUBLIC-PRIVATE PARTNERSHIPS IN HOUSING
http://www.cmhc-schl.gc.ca/Centres/Partner/partner.html

CMHC SPEAKERS BUREAU
http://www.cmhc-schl.gc.ca/Community/speakers.html

CMHC OFFICE IN FREDERICTON, N.B.
http://www.cygnus.nb.ca/cmhc/cmhc_hme.html

SEND YOUR COMMENTS
Email: cmhcinfo@nbnet.nb.ca

CMHC OFFICE IN TORONTO, ONTARIO
http://www.aecinfo.com/cmhc/
Email: eborkows@cmhc.e-mail.com

CMHC OFFICE IN VICTORIA, B.C.
http://www.islandnet.com/~cmhcvic/homepage.html
Email: cmhcvic@cmhc-schl.gc.ca

Canada–Newfoundland Offshore Petroleum Board

http://canada.gc.ca/depts/agencies/cnpind_e.html

The Canada-Newfoundland Offshore Petroleum Board is a regulatory body with jurisdiction within the Newfoundland Offshore area.

This site is not yet fully developed at the time of publication of this book and offers limited information pertaining to the board's mandate and field of responsibility.

Canada–Nova Scotia Offshore Petroleum Board Office

http://Fox.nstn.ca/~cnsopb/

ORGANIZATION CHART
http://Fox.nstn.ca/~cnsopb/org.html

BOARD MEMBERS
http://Fox.nstn.ca/~cnsopb/members.html

STAFF
(Including responsibilities and email addresses)
http://Fox.nstn.ca/~cnsopb/staff3.html

CORE AND DATA ARCHIVE LAB
http://Fox.nstn.ca/~cnsopb/lab.html

MAP OF JURISDICTION
http://Fox.nstn.ca/~cnsopb/area.html

PUBLICATIONS
http://Fox.nstn.ca/~cnsopb/list.html

OWNERSHIP SUMMARY OF ALL OFFSHORE INTERESTS
http://Fox.nstn.ca/~cnsopb/interest1.html

SEND YOUR COMMENTS
Email: bsmith@cnsopb.ns.ca

Canada Pension Plan Consultations

http://www.cpp.rpc.gc.ca/homepage.htm

GENERAL INFORMATION
http://www.cpp.rpc.gc.ca/backgr/gene.htm

SCHEDULE OF PUBLIC MEETINGS
http://www.cpp.rpc.gc.ca/datese.htm

NEWS RELEASES
http://www.cpp.rpc.gc.ca/news/newse.htm

PUBLICATION
http://www.cpp.rpc.gc.ca/maindoc/toce.htm

Canada Ports Corporation

http://canada.gc.ca/depts/agencies/cpoind_e.html

The Canada Ports Corporation is responsible for a number of ports across the country.

This site is not yet fully developed at the time of publication of this book and offers limited information pertaining to the corporation's mandate and field of responsibility.

Canada Post Corporation

http://www.mailposte.ca/

CORPORATE OVERVIEW
http://www.mailposte.ca/english/overview/overview.html

ORIGINS, HISTORY, MILESTONES, SIZE AND SCOPE, ETC.
Table of Contents
http://www.mailposte.ca/english/enghome.html

WHAT'S NEW
(News releases/archive/speeches)
http://www.mailposte.ca/english/whatsnew/whatsnew.html

POSTAL CODE LOOKUP
http://www.mailposte.ca/english/pclookup/pclookup.html

POSTAL SERVICES
http://www.mailposte.ca/english/postservice/postsrv.html

POSTAL RATES
http://www.mailposte.ca/english/postrate/postrate.html

FOR STAMP COLLECTORS
http://www.mailposte.ca/english/stamp/stamp.html

Catalogue
http://www.mailposte.ca/english/stamp/catalog.html

What's New
http://www.mailposte.ca/english/stamp/new.html

Philately Links Around the World
http://www.mailposte.ca/english/stamp/hotlink.html

Order Information
http://www.mailposte.ca/english/stamp/order.html

POST OFFICE LOCATIONS
http://www.mailposte.ca/english/polocation/location.html

ELECTRONIC SERVICES
http://www.mailposte.ca/english/electronic/electronic.html

HYBRID MAIL
http://www.mailposte.ca/english/electronic/hybrid.html

ELECTRONIC COMMERCE
http://www.mailposte.ca/english/electronic/electronicom.html

DOCUMENT ON DEMAND
http://www.mailposte.ca/english/electronic/docu.html

SALES AND SERVICE
(Services, addresses, and telephone numbers)
http://www.mailposte.ca/english/saleservice/salserv.html

BUSINESS CENTRE
(Two locations: Calgary, Alberta, and London, Ontario)
http://www.mailposte.ca/english/smallbus/smallbus.html

DIRECT MARKETING CENTRE
(Connexions)
http://www.mailposte.ca/english/directmarketing/connexions/connexions.html

What Is It?
http://www.mailposte.ca/english/directmarketing/connexions/aboutconnex.html

Direct Marketing Guide
http://www.mailposte.ca/english/directmarketing/connexions/about.html

How to Reach Them
Email: answers@connex.ca

HOTLINKS
(Search engines, foreign postal agencies, collecting links, and more)
http://www.mailposte.ca/english/hotlinks/hotlinks.html

SEND YOUR COMMENTS
Email: service@mailposte.ca

CANADA POST MANDATE REVIEW
http://canada.gc.ca/cpmr-emscp/main.html

Terms of Reference
http://canada.gc.ca/cpmr-emscp/refer_e.html

Public Meetings
http://canada.gc.ca/cpmr-emscp/meet_e.html

Submissions
http://canada.gc.ca/cpmr-emscp/sub_e.html

Contact Information
http://canada.gc.ca/cpmr-emscp/conta_e.html

Canadian Artists and Producers Professional Relations Tribunal

http://homer.ic.gc.ca/capprt/capprt_e.html

ABOUT THE TRIBUNAL
http://homer.ic.gc.ca/capprt/about_e.html

CURRENT NEWS
http://homer.ic.gc.ca/capprt/notices/notice_e.html

STATUS OF THE ARTIST ACT
http://homer.ic.gc.ca/capprt/act_e.html

TRIBUNAL PROCEDURES
http://homer.ic.gc.ca/capprt/pguide_e.html

TRIBUNAL DECISIONS
http://homer.ic.gc.ca/capprt/tribun_e.html

ARCHIVES
http://homer.ic.gc.ca/capprt/notices/archive.html

MAILING LIST
http://homer.ic.gc.ca/capprt/mail_e.html

CERTIFICATION REGISTER
http://homer.ic.gc.ca/capprt/regis_e.html

Canadian Broadcasting Corporation

http://www.cbc.ca/

ABOUT CBC
http://www.cbc.ca/aboutcbc/aboutcbc.html

MANDATE
http://www.cbc.ca/aboutcbc/mandate/mandate.html

FACTS
http://www.cbc.ca/aboutcbc/factfile/factfile.html

HISTORY
http://radioworks.cbc.ca/radio/bcentre/cbc-history.html

CBC WEBMAP
(Operations chart with hotlinks)
http://www.cbc.ca/commnhtm/webmap.html

CBC EMAIL ADDRESSES
(Administration, radio, TV, 200+ addresses)
http://www.cbc.ca/aboutcbc/address/address.html

CBC WEBSITES AND NEWSGROUPS
(Site-specific for various shows, personalities, and locations)
http://www.cbc.ca/moresite/moresite.html

THE NATIONAL TRANSCRIPTS ONLINE
http://www.cbc.ca/sites/ptn/ptn.html

NEWSGROUPS
CBC Television
alt.tv.networks.cbc

Royal Canadian Air Farce
alt.comedy.air-farce

CBC Radio
alt.radio.networks.cbc

WHAT'S NEW
http://www.cbc.ca/whatsnew/whatsnew.html

PRESIDENT'S SPEECHES
http://www.cbc.ca/aboutcbc/speech/speech.html

AUDITOR GENERAL'S REPORT ON CBC
http://www.cbc.ca/aboutcbc/audgen.html

MANDATE REVIEW COMMITTEE
(CBC, NFB, and Telefilm Canada)
http://edie.cprost.sfu.ca/~paul/

PUBLIC FEEDBACK
http://www.cbc.ca/aboutcbc/feedback/feedback.html

MEDIA ACCOUNTABILITY
http://www.cbc.ca/aboutcbc/mediaacc/mediaacc.html

CBC OMBUDSMAN
Quicktime Movie
(Video for Windows)
http://www.cbc.ca/video/ombudsmn.avi

CBC ENGLISH TELEVISION
http://www.cbc.ca/tv/

Movies, Specials, and New Programming
http://www.cbc.ca/tv/launch/launch.html

Olympic Coverage
http://www.cbc.ca/olympics/

TV Schedule
http://www.cbc.ca/tv/schedule/schedule.html

CBC Celebrities
(Some with video files)
http://www.cbc.ca/tv/celebs/celebs.html

VIDEO ARCHIVES
http://www.cbc.ca/tv/vault/vault.html

LIST OF STATIONS ACROSS CANADA
(With clickable map)
http://www.cbc.ca/tv/regions/regions.html

ARTS, MUSIC, SCIENCE, AND VARIETY PROGRAMMING
http://www.cbc.ca/tv/amsv/amsv.html

COMEDY AND DRAMATIC SERIES PROGRAMMING
http://www.cbc.ca/tv/comdram/comdram.html

CHILDREN'S PROGRAMMING
http://www.cbc.ca/tv/pground/pground.html

DAYTIME PROGRAMMING
http://www.cbc.ca/tv/daytime/daytime.html

NEWS AND CURRENT AFFAIRS
http://www.cbc.ca/tv/newsca/newsca.html

SPORTS
http://www.cbc.ca/tv/sports/sports.html

WEEKEND
http://www.cbc.ca/tv/weekend/weekend.html

REGIONAL
http://www.cbc.ca/tv/regional/regional.html

CBC RADIO
(With links to CBC Radio & Stereo programs)
http://www.radio.cbc.ca/

REGIONAL PROGRAMMING
http://www.radio.cbc.ca/radio/regional/index.html

CBC RADIO NEWS
(With staff and show info, and two daily audio newscasts online)
http://www.radio.cbc.ca/radio/programs/news/news.html

CBC SPORTS
(Audio reports, info about sports reporters)
http://www.radio.cbc.ca/radio/programs/sports/sports.html

CBC RADIO DRAMA
(With links to drama programs: Between the Covers, Mystery Project, Sunday Showcase)
http://www.radio.cbc.ca/radio/programs/drama/drama.html

SCRIPTWRITER'S KIT
(Instructions, contact list, etc.)
http://www.radio.cbc.ca/radio/programs/drama/writers.html

THE TILDEN CANADIAN LITERARY AWARDS
(Rules and regulations)
http://www.radio.cbc.ca/radio/programs/drama/tilden.html

AUDIO TOOLS
(With audio players to download for your computer)
http://www.radio.cbc.ca/radio/tools/tools.html

CBC NEWSWORLD
http://www.cbc.ca/nw/nw.html

SOCIÉTÉ RADIO CANADA
(CBC French services)
http://www.src-mtl.com/

RADIO CANADA INTERNATIONAL
http://www.radio.cbc.ca/radio/rci/rci.html

Send Your Comments
Email: rci@montreal.src.ca

CBC NORTH POLE PROJECT
http://www.cbc.ca/aboutcbc/npole/npole.html
Contains the first digital photos ever from the North Pole

ALPHABETICAL LISTING OF ALL CBC WEBSITES

http://www.cbc.ca/commnhtm/hotlinks.html

INTERNATIONAL BROADCASTING HOTLIST

(Public broadcasters around the world)
http://www.cbc.ca/aboutcbc/bclinks/bclinks.html

SEND YOUR COMMENTS

Email: cbcinput@toronto.cbc.ca

Canadian Centre for Management Development

http://canada.gc.ca/depts/agencies/cmdind_e.html

The Canadian Centre for Management Development fosters excellence in teaching and research in public sector management.

This site is not yet fully developed at the time of publication of this book and offers limited information pertaining to the centre's mandate and field of responsibility.

Canadian Centre for Occupational Health and Safety

http://www.ccohs.ca

ABOUT CCOHS PRODUCTS AND SERVICES
http://www.ccohs.ca/CCOHS/products.html

AVAILABLE CCOHS COURSES
http://www.ccohs.ca/CCOHS/courses.html

DEMONSTRATIONS OF CCOHS CD-ROM PRODUCTS
http://www.ccohs.ca/CCOHS/demos.html

CUSTOMER SERVICE
Email: custserv@ccohs.ca

Canadian Commercial Corporation

http://www.ccc.ca/

VIRTUAL TRADE PLAZA
http://www.ccc.ca/index-e.html

WHAT IS THE CCC?
http://www.ccc.ca/whatis.html

PROGRAMS
http://www.ccc.ca/work.html

PROGRESS PAYMENT PROGRAM
http://www.ccc.ca/progress.html

FOR U.S. MARKETS
http://www.ccc.ca/usmark-e.html

WORLDWIDE SERVICES
http://www.ccc.ca/wdmark-e.html

UNITED NATIONS SALES
http://www.ccc.ca/unsale-e.html

SMALL- AND MEDIUM-SIZED ENTERPRISES
http://www.ccc.ca/sme-e.html

LARGER CORPORATIONS
http://www.ccc.ca/larcor-e.html

ADVANTAGES FOR CANADIAN EXPORTERS
http://www.ccc.ca/canex-e.html

ADVANTAGES FOR FOREIGN CUSTOMERS
http://www.ccc.ca/forbuy-e.html
(Contains audio speech excerpts)
http://www.ccc.ca/result.html

NEWS
http://www.ccc.ca/flash.html

CCC'S 50TH ANNIVERSARY
http://www.ccc.ca/anniv-e.html

SELECTED STAFF MEMBERS
http://www.ccc.ca/people.html

TRADE LINKS AROUND THE WORLD
http://www.ccc.ca/links.html

This site features an excellent hotlist of key trade-related sites in both public and private sectors.

CCC CONTACTS
http://www.ccc.ca/contact.html

SEND YOUR COMMENTS
Email: info@ccc.ca

Canadian Cultural Property Export Review Board

http://canada.gc.ca/depts/agencies/cpeind_e.html

The Canadian Cultural Property Export Review Board's mandate is to preserve Canadian heritage in Canada.

This site is not yet fully developed at the time of publication of this book and offers limited information pertaining to the board's mandate and field of responsibility.

Canadian Dairy Commission

http://www.agr.ca/cdc

ABOUT CDC
http://aceis.agr.ca/cdc/weare.html

POLICIES AND PROGRAMS
http://aceis.agr.ca/cdc/policy.html

PRESS RELEASES
http://aceis.agr.ca/cdc/press.html

UPCOMING MEETINGS AND EVENTS
http://aceis.agr.ca/cdc/notice.html

HOTLINKS
http://aceis.agr.ca/cdc/cdcsites.html

SEND YOUR COMMENTS
Email: sperron@em.agr.ca

Canadian Environmental Assessment Agency

http://www.ceaa.gc.ca

WHAT IT IS
http://www.ceaa.gc.ca/english/agency/

MISSION STATEMENT
http://www.ceaa.gc.ca/english/agency/mission.html

STAFF
http://www.ceaa.gc.ca/english/agency/staf_dir.html

LEGISLATION
http://www.ceaa.gc.ca/english/act/

PUBLIC REGISTRY SYSTEM
http://www.ceaa.gc.ca/english/pub_reg/pubreg.htm

FEDERAL ENVIRONMENTAL ASSESSMENT INDEX
http://www.ceaa.gc.ca/english/pub_reg/feaindex.html

By Province or Territory
http://www.ceaa.gc.ca/registry/english/by_province.html

By Responsible Authority
http://www.ceaa.gc.ca/registry/english/by_department.html

By Drainage Region
http://www.ceaa.gc.ca/registry/english/by_drainage_region.html

By Ecozone
http://www.ceaa.gc.ca/registry/english/by_ecozone.html

Outside Canada
http://www.ceaa.gc.ca/registry/english/by_foreign_country.html

RESPONSIBLE AUTHORITY'S GUIDE
http://www.ceaa.gc.ca/english/info_hld/ra_guide/ra_guide.html

AVAILABLE AGENCY DOCUMENTS
http://www.ceaa.gc.ca/english/info_hld/info.html

FEDERAL–PROVINCIAL AGREEMENTS
http://www.ceaa.gc.ca/english/act/fedp.html

HOTLINKS
http://www.ceaa.gc.ca/english/othersrc/

SEND YOUR COMMENTS
Email: aray@gsro.carleton.ca

Canadian Film Development Corporation

http://canada.gc.ca/depts/agencies/cfdind_e.html

The Canadian Film Development Corporation is better known as Telefilm Canada.

This site is not yet fully developed at the time of publication of this book and offers limited information pertaining to the corporation's mandate and field of responsibility.

Canadian Forest Service

http://nrcan.gc.ca/cfs/index.html

MANDATE
http://nrcan.gc.ca/cfs/mandat/mandat_e.html

WHAT'S NEW
http://nrcan.gc.ca/cfs/new/new_e.html

PROGRAMS AND ACTIVITIES
http://nrcan.gc.ca/cfs/proj/proj_e.html

PUBLICATIONS
http://nrcan.gc.ca/cfs/pub/pub_e.html

Canadian Heritage

http://www.pch.gc.ca/

HOMEPAGE
http://www.pch.gc.ca/home.html

CONTENTS
http://www.pch.gc.ca/pch/intro-e.html

WHAT'S NEW
http://www.pch.gc.ca/pch/whatsnew.html

CITIZENSHIP AND CANADIAN IDENTITY
http://www.pch.gc.ca/pch/sectors/dch-1-e.html

CULTURAL DEVELOPMENT AND HERITAGE
http://www.pch.gc.ca/pch/sectors/dch-2-e.html

Canadian Heritage Information Network
http://www.chin.gc.ca/

Send Your Comments
Email : service@chin.gc.ca

What's New
http://www.chin.gc.ca/CHIN/General/e_what.html

About CHIN
http://www.chin.gc.ca/CHIN/General/e_general.html

Heritage Information
http://www.chin.gc.ca/CHIN/Resources/e_resources.html

Products and Services
(Training, publications, and multimedia products)
http://www.chin.gc.ca/CHIN/Products/e_products.html

Feedback
http://www.chin.gc.ca/CHIN/General/e_feedback.html

PARKS CANADA
http://parkscanada.pch.gc.ca/

Send Your Comments
Email: Parks_Webmaster@pch.gc.ca

National Historic Sites
http://parkscanada.pch.gc.ca/parks/nhsdemo.htm

Clickable Map
http://parkscanada.pch.gc.ca/parks/can_nhse.htm

Alphabetical List by Province
http://parkscanada.pch.gc.ca/parks/alphae.htm

National Parks
http://parkscanada.pch.gc.ca/parks/npdemo.htm

Clickable Map
http://parkscanada.pch.gc.ca/parks/can_npe.htm

Alphabetical List by Province
http://parkscanada.pch.gc.ca/parks/alphap2e.htm

CORPORATE SERVICES
http://www.pch.gc.ca/pch/sectors/dch-4-e.html

ADDRESSES
http://www.pch.gc.ca/pch/addresse.html

LISTING OF RELATED AGENCIES AND CORPORATIONS
http://www.pch.gc.ca/pch/agencies.html

SEND YOUR COMMENTS
Email: Richard_Caron@pch.gc.ca

Canadian Human Rights Commission

http://www.chrc.ca/

NEWS RELEASES
http://www.chrc.ca/frames/releases.htm

ANNUAL REPORT
http://www.chrc.ca/ar1995/contents.htm

HUMAN RIGHTS FORUM
http://www.chrc.ca/frames/forum.htm

REFERENCE LIBRARY
http://www.chrc.ca/frames/docs.htm

CANADIAN HUMAN RIGHTS ACT
http://www.chrc.ca/chra.html

RELATED HUMAN RIGHTS LINKS
http://www.chrc.ca/frames/links.htm

CONTACTS
http://www.chrc.ca/frames/offices.htm

SEND YOUR COMMENTS
Email: info@chrc.ca

Canadian Intergovernmental Conference Secretariat

http://canada.gc.ca/depts/agencies/cicind_e.html

The CICS provides services to meetings of ministers and deputy ministers and for the planning and conduct of federal–provincial and interprovincial conferences.

This site is not yet fully developed at the time of publication of this book and offers limited information pertaining to the secretariat's mandate and field of responsibility.

Canadian International Development Agency

http://www.acdi-cida.gc.ca/

TABLE OF CONTENTS
http://www.acdi-cida.gc.ca/index_e.htm

WHAT'S NEW
http://www.acdi-cida.gc.ca/cida_in/enew.htm

PRESS RELEASES
http://www.acdi-cida.gc.ca/cida_in/epressr.htm

PUBLICATIONS
http://www.acdi-cida.gc.ca/publicat/index_e.htm

SPEECHES
http://www.acdi-cida.gc.ca/cida_in/espeech.htm

MANDATE
http://www.acdi-cida.gc.ca/mandate/index_e.htm

SECTORS OF INTERVENTION
http://www.acdi-cida.gc.ca/cida_in/esector.htm

PROGRAMS
http://www.acdi-cida.gc.ca/cida_in/eprogram.htm

PROGRAM BRANCHES
http://www.acdi-cida.gc.ca/operatin/index_e.htm

SERVICE BRANCHES
http://www.acdi-cida.gc.ca/branch/index_e.htm

HOW TO DO BUSINESS WITH CIDA
http://www.acdi-cida.gc.ca/faq/involv_e.htm

Industrial Cooperation Program
http://www.acdi-cida.gc.ca/cida_in/einc.htm

Development Information Program
http://www.acdi-cida.gc.ca/service/communic/dip_e.htm

PUBLIC CONSULTATIONS
http://www.acdi-cida.gc.ca/cida_in/econsult.htm

RELATED LINKS
http://www.acdi-cida.gc.ca/other_e.htm

Canadian International Trade Tribunal

http://canada.gc.ca/depts/agencies/cttind_e.html

The Canadian International Trade Tribunal is responsible for conducting anti-dumping and countervailing injury inquiries.

This site is not yet fully developed at the time of publication of this book and offers limited information pertaining to the tribunal's mandate and field of responsibility.

Canadian Museum of Civilization

http://www.cmcc.muse.digital.ca/cmc/cmceng/welcmeng.html

WHAT'S NEW
http://www.cmcc.muse.digital.ca/cmc/cmceng/neweng.html

ABOUT THE MUSEUM
http://www.cmcc.muse.digital.ca/cmc/cmceng/introeng.html

General Info
(Location map, address, telephone number, operating hours, fees)
http://www.cmcc.muse.digital.ca/cmc/cmceng/genereng.html

The Museum's Architecture
http://www.cmcc.muse.digital.ca/cmc/cmceng/archieng.html

Mandate
http://www.cmcc.muse.digital.ca/cmc/cmceng/ipurpeng.html

Strategic Plan
http://www.cmcc.muse.digital.ca/cmc/cmceng/strateng.html

History
http://www.cmcc.muse.digital.ca/cmc/cmceng/ihisteng.html

Cyberboutique
http://www.cmcc.muse.digital.ca/cgi-bin/cmc.cgi

EVENTS CALENDAR
http://www.cmcc.muse.digital.ca/cmc/cmceng/caleng.html

ONLINE GALLERY TOUR
http://www.cmcc.muse.digital.ca/cmc/cmceng/exhibeng.html

CHILDREN'S MUSEUM
http://www.cmcc.muse.digital.ca/cmc/cmceng/cmeng.html

PROGRAMS, SERVICES, AND FACILITIES
http://www.cmcc.muse.digital.ca/cmc/cmceng/facileng.html

Information Services
http://www.cmcc.muse.digital.ca/cmc/cmceng/infoeng.html

Special Events
http://www.cmcc.muse.digital.ca/cmc/cmceng/eventeng.html

Films
http://www.cmcc.muse.digital.ca/cmc/cmceng/filmeng.html

Lectures
http://www.cmcc.muse.digital.ca/cmc/cmceng/lecteng.html

Live Performances
http://www.cmcc.muse.digital.ca/cmc/cmceng/liveeng.html

Festivals
http://www.cmcc.muse.digital.ca/cmc/cmceng/festeng.html

Theatre Company
http://www.cmcc.muse.digital.ca/cmc/cmceng/theateng.html

Cineplus IMAX
http://www.cmcc.muse.digital.ca/cmc/cmceng/cinepeng.html

Group Services
http://www.cmcc.muse.digital.ca/cmc/cmceng/groupeng.html

School Services
http://www.cmcc.muse.digital.ca/cmc/cmceng/schooeng.html

Library and Archives
http://www.cmcc.muse.digital.ca/cmc/cmceng/libreng.html

Collections
http://www.cmcc.muse.digital.ca/cmc/cmceng/libcoeng.html

How to Reach Them
Email: library@cmcc.muse.digital.ca

Food Services
http://www.cmcc.muse.digital.ca/cmc/cmceng/foodeng.html

Facility Rentals
http://www.cmcc.muse.digital.ca/cmc/cmceng/renteng.html

Special Needs Services
http://www.cmcc.muse.digital.ca/cmc/cmceng/specieng.html

MUSEUM COLLECTIONS
http://www.cmcc.muse.digital.ca/cmc/cmceng/colleng.html

Digitization Project
http://www.cmcc.muse.digital.ca/cmc/cmceng/digiteng.html

RESEARCH ACTIVITIES AND VISITOR STUDIES
http://www.cmcc.muse.digital.ca/cmc/cmceng/behineng.html

HOW TO SUPPORT THE MUSEUM
http://www.cmcc.muse.digital.ca/cmc/cmceng/getineng.html

NATIONAL POSTAL MUSEUM
http://www.cmcc.muse.digital.ca/cmc/cmceng/npmeng.html

Educational Programs
http://www.cmcc.muse.digital.ca/cmc/cmceng/npmeeng.html

Canadian Museum of Nature

http://canada.gc.ca/depts/agencies/cmnind_e.html

This site is not yet fully developed at the time of publication of this book and offers limited information pertaining to the museum's mandate and field of responsibility.

Canadian Polar Commission

http://www.polarcom.gc.ca/index.html

MEMBERS
http://www.polarcom.gc.ca/members.html

OFFICES
http://www.polarcom.gc.ca/offices.html

CANADIAN POLAR COMMISSION ACT
http://www.polarcom.gc.ca/comm.html

PUBLICATIONS
http://www.polarcom.gc.ca/publications.html

HOTLINKS
http://www.polarcom.gc.ca/interest.html

FEEDBACK
http://www.polarcom.gc.ca/feedback.html

"FOR GENERATIONS TO COME" CONFERENCE
(Fall 1996)
http://www.polarcom.gc.ca/confer1.html

Canadian Radio-Television and Telecommunications Commission

http://www.crtc.gc.ca/

TABLE OF CONTENTS
http://www.crtc.gc.ca/eng/english.htm

WHAT'S NEW
http://www.crtc.gc.ca/eng/news/whatsnew.htm

UPCOMING
http://www.crtc.gc.ca/eng/news/coming.htm

ABOUT THE CRTC
http://www.crtc.gc.ca/eng/backgrnd/whatgood.htm

ORGANIZATION CHART
http://www.crtc.gc.ca/images/org_e.gif

TELEPHONE NUMBERS
http://www.crtc.gc.ca/eng/backgrnd/infoshee.htm

CRTC COMMISSIONERS
http://www.crtc.gc.ca/eng/backgrnd/g2e.htm

HAVING YOUR SAY
http://www.crtc.gc.ca/eng/info_sht/g6e.htm

FILING A BROADCASTING COMPLAINT
http://www.crtc.gc.ca/eng/info_sht/g8e.htm

FILING A TELECOMMUNICATIONS COMPLAINT
http://www.crtc.gc.ca/eng/backgrnd/tcompe.htm

GENERAL INFORMATION
http://www.crtc.gc.ca/eng/topics/general.htm

CONTACTING THE CRTC
http://www.crtc.gc.ca/eng/info_sht/g1e.htm

PROGRAM PRIORITIES AND EXPENDITURES
http://www.crtc.gc.ca/eng/info_sht/g10e.htm

BROADCASTING INFORMATION
http://www.crtc.gc.ca/eng/topics/bcasting.htm

FILING A BROADCASTING INTERVENTION
http://www.crtc.gc.ca/eng/info_sht/g4e.htm

LOUD COMMERCIALS
http://www.crtc.gc.ca/eng/info_sht/g3e.htm

DIRECT TO HOME POLICY
http://www.crtc.gc.ca/eng/info_sht/g7ae.htm

CANADIAN CONTENT
http://www.crtc.gc.ca/eng/info_sht/g11e.htm

CABLE
http://www.crtc.gc.ca/eng/info_sht/cps1e.htm

Distribution
http://www.crtc.gc.ca/eng/info_sht/cdbt4e.htm

Specialty and Pay-TV
http://www.crtc.gc.ca/eng/info_sht/cdbt5e.htm

Digital and Pick & Pay Cable Service
http://www.crtc.gc.ca/eng/info_sht/cdbt6e.htm

Implementation Schedule
http://www.crtc.gc.ca/images/cdbt6ea.jpg

How Are Cable Rates Set?
http://www.crtc.gc.ca/eng/info_sht/cdbt7e.htm

Glossary of Cable Terms
http://www.crtc.gc.ca/eng/info_sht/cdbt8e.htm

About Cable Billing
http://www.crtc.gc.ca/eng/info_sht/cdbt11e.htm

Signal Substitution
http://www.crtc.gc.ca/eng/info_sht/cdbt10e.htm

The Facts About Home Satellite Broadcasting
http://www.crtc.gc.ca/eng/info_sht/bdt13e.htm

About the Notice to Cable Subscribers
http://www.crtc.gc.ca/eng/info_sht/bdt12e.htm

RADIO
About the MAPL System
http://www.crtc.gc.ca/eng/info_sht/r1e.htm

TELEVISION
About Violence on TV
http://www.crtc.gc.ca/eng/info_sht/tv1e.htm

The Canadian Program Production Fund
http://www.crtc.gc.ca/eng/info_sht/tv2e.htm

About New Specialty and Pay-TV Channels
http://www.crtc.gc.ca/eng/info_sht/tv3e.htm

Benefits for Consumers and the Creative Community
http://www.crtc.gc.ca/eng/info_sht/tv4e.htm

TELECOMMUNICATIONS
http://www.crtc.gc.ca/eng/topics/telecom.htm

Taxation Guidelines
http://www.crtc.gc.ca/eng/topics/telecom/taxation.htm

PRICE REGULATION FRAMEWORK
http://www.crtc.gc.ca/eng/info_sht/t1e.htm

Equitable Pricing
http://www.crtc.gc.ca/eng/info_sht/t2e.htm

Safeguards for Consumers and Competitors
http://www.crtc.gc.ca/eng/info_sht/t3e.htm

Competitive Opportunities
http://www.crtc.gc.ca/eng/info_sht/t4e.htm

About Convergence
http://www.crtc.gc.ca/eng/info_sht/t5e.htm

Forbearance
http://www.crtc.gc.ca/eng/info_sht/t6e.htm

New Regulatory Framework
http://www.crtc.gc.ca/eng/info_sht/t7e.htm

Glossary
http://www.crtc.gc.ca/eng/info_sht/t8e.htm

INFORMATION HIGHWAY
http://www.crtc.gc.ca/eng/topics/infohigh.htm

Competition and Culture on Canada's Information Highway
http://www.crtc.gc.ca/eng/highway/hwy9505e.htm

REPORT OF THE CRTC PROCEEDING
http://www.crtc.gc.ca/eng/info_sht/g9e.htm

COMMENTS RECEIVED BY THE CRTC
http://www.crtc.gc.ca/eng/highway/comment.htm

LEGISLATION
Canadian Radio-Television and Telecommunications Commission Act
http://www.crtc.gc.ca/eng/legal/crtc_e.htm

Broadcasting Act
http://www.crtc.gc.ca/eng/legal/broad_e.htm

Telecommunications Act
http://www.crtc.gc.ca/eng/legal/telecome.htm

Rules of Procedure

Broadcasting
http://www.crtc.gc.ca/eng/legal/brodacte.htm

Telecommunications
http://www.crtc.gc.ca/eng/legal/teleacte.htm

SOCIAL ISSUES

Gender Portrayal
http://www.crtc.gc.ca/eng/social/92-58.htm

Employment Equity
http://www.crtc.gc.ca/eng/social/92-59.htm

TV Violence
http://www.crtc.gc.ca/eng/social/tv.htm

Telecommunications Pilot Projects
http://www.crtc.gc.ca/eng/pilot/telecom/telpilot.htm

Archives

Broadcasting
http://www.crtc.gc.ca/eng/pilot/telecom/telpilot.htm

Telecommunications
http://www.crtc.gc.ca/eng/pilot/telecom/telpilot.htm

SEND YOUR COMMENTS

Email: info@crtc.x400.gc.ca

Canadian Security Intelligence Service

http://www.csis-scrs.gc.ca/

WHAT'S NEW
http://www.csis-scrs.gc.ca/eng/new/whatnewe.html

THE CSIS ACT
http://www.csis-scrs.gc.ca/eng/act/csisacte.html

ABOUT CSIS
http://www.csis-scrs.gc.ca/eng/menu/aboute.html

PUBLIC REPORTS
http://www.csis-scrs.gc.ca/eng/publicrp/pubrepse.html

COMMENTARY SERIES
http://www.csis-scrs.gc.ca/eng/comment/comsume.html

CSIS ADDRESSES AND PHONE NUMBERS
http://www.csis-scrs.gc.ca/eng/address/contacte.html

Canadian War Museum

http://www.cmcc.muse.digital.ca/cwm/cwmeng/cwmeng.html

GENERAL INFORMATION
(Address, fees, hours of operation, etc.)
http://www.cmcc.muse.digital.ca/cwm/cwmeng/cwmgieng.html

HISTORY AND MISSION
http://www.cmcc.muse.digital.ca/cwm/cwmeng/cwmhieng.html

EXHIBITIONS
http://www.cmcc.muse.digital.ca/cwm/cwmeng/cwmexeng.html

PROGRAMS, FACILITIES, AND SERVICES
http://www.cmcc.muse.digital.ca/cwm/cwmeng/cwmppeng.html

MULTIMEDIA PRODUCTS
http://www.cmcc.muse.digital.ca/cwm/cwmeng/cwmmmeng.html

CYBERBOUTIQUE
http://www.cmcc.muse.digital.ca/cgi-bin/cmc.cgi

EDUCATION PROGRAM
http://www.cmcc.muse.digital.ca/cwm/cwmeng/cwmedeng.html

MUSEUM COLLECTIONS
http://www.cmcc.muse.digital.ca/cwm/cwmeng/cwmcoeng.html

BECOMING A FRIEND OF THE MUSEUM
http://www.cmcc.muse.digital.ca/cwm/cwmeng/cwmfreng.html

Canadian Wheat Board

http://canada.gc.ca/depts/agencies/cwbind_e.html

This site is not yet fully developed at the time of publication of this book and offers limited information pertaining to the board's mandate and field of responsibility.

Citizenship and Immigration Canada

http://cicnet.ingenia.com/

TABLE OF CONTENTS
http://cicnet.ingenia.com/english/index.html

WHAT'S NEW
http://cicnet.ingenia.com/english/whatsnew.html

ABOUT THE DEPARTMENT
http://cicnet.ingenia.com/english/cicinfo/corpbroc.html

ABOUT CANADIAN CITIZENSHIP
http://cicnet.ingenia.com/english/cicinfo/corpbroc.html

ABOUT BECOMING A CANADIAN CITIZEN
http://cicnet.ingenia.com/english/howto/citizen1.html

WHAT TO DO TO BECOME A CITIZEN
http://cicnet.ingenia.com/english/howto/citizen2.html

ABOUT CITIZENSHIP REGISTRATION
http://cicnet.ingenia.com/english/cicinfo/registr.html

OPERATIONS
International
http://cicnet.ingenia.com/english/cicinfo/intserv.html

National
http://cicnet.ingenia.com/english/cicinfo/natserv.html

PRIVATE SPONSORSHIP OF REFUGEES
http://cicnet.ingenia.com/english/new/sponsore.html

SERVING CANADIANS
http://cicnet.ingenia.com/english/cicinfo/hilights.html

CONTACTS
http://cicnet.ingenia.com/english/cicinfo/moreinfo.html

PUBLICATIONS
http://cicnet.ingenia.com/english/publicat/publicat.html

RESEARCH
http://cicnet.ingenia.com/english/research.html

OFFICES ABROAD
http://cicnet.ingenia.com/english/pubs/ptsabrd/ptsabrd.html

OFFICES IN CANADA
http://cicnet.ingenia.com/english/regions/cice.html

Commissioner of Official Languages

http://canada.gc.ca/depts/agencies/olloeind/html

ANNUAL REPORT
http://canada.gc.ca/depts/agencies/ar95-e.pdf

Consulting and Audit Canada

http://w3.pwgsc.gc.ca/cac/

WHAT'S NEW
http://w3.pwgsc.gc.ca/cac/text/whaeng.htm

SERVICES
http://w3.pwgsc.gc.ca/cac/text/sereng.htm

FOCUS
http://w3.pwgsc.gc.ca/cac/text/foceng.htm

OFFICE LOCATIONS
http://w3.pwgsc.gc.ca/cac/text/offeng.htm

OPTIMUM — THE JOURNAL OF PUBLIC-SECTOR MANAGEMENT
http://w3.pwgsc.gc.ca/cac/text/opteng.htm

Copyright Board Canada

http://www.gc.ca/copyright_board/english.htm

The Copyright Board focuses on issues relating to the public performance of music.

This site is not yet fully developed at the time of publication of this book and offers limited information pertaining to the board's mandate and field of responsibility.

Correctional Investigator Canada

http://canada.gc.ca/depts/agencies/ociind_e.html

The Correctional Investigator investigates and reports on the problems of inmates in Canada.

This site is not yet fully developed at the time of publication of this book and offers limited information pertaining to the investigator's mandate and field of responsibility.

Correctional Service Canada

http://www.csc-scc.gc.ca/

OFFICE OF THE COMMISSIONER
http://198.103.98.138/commish/

CORRECTIONAL RESEARCH AND DEVELOPMENT — PUBLICATIONS
http://198.103.98.138/crd/

COMMUNITY CORRECTIONS
http://198.103.98.138/cacc/

INTERGOVERNMENTAL AFFAIRS
http://198.103.98.138/iga/

SEND YOUR COMMENTS
Email: agraham@magi.com

Defence Construction Canada

http://canada.gc.ca/depts/agencies/dccind_e.html

Defence Construction Canada is an agency which oversees military construction and maintenance projects for the Department of National Defence.

This site is not yet fully developed at the time of publication of this book and offers limited information pertaining to the agency's mandate and field of responsibility.

Department of Finance

http://www.fin.gc.ca/

THE HON. PAUL MARTIN, MINISTER
http://www.fin.gc.ca/minfine.html

SEND YOUR COMMENTS
http://www.fin.gc.ca/commente/commen_e.html

TABLE OF CONTENTS
http://www.fin.gc.ca/fin-eng.html

NEWS RELEASES
http://www.fin.gc.ca/newse96/newse.html

SPEECHES
http://www.fin.gc.ca/newse96/speeche.html

ABOUT THE DEPARTMENT
http://www.fin.gc.ca/fininfoe.html

DEPARTMENTAL PUBLICATIONS
Subscription Series
http://www.fin.gc.ca/subs96/subse.html

At No Cost
http://www.fin.gc.ca/freepube.html

Download Economic and Fiscal Update
http://www.fin.gc.ca/updatee/updatee.pdf

Facts About the Canadian Financial System
http://www.fin.gc.ca/fctsheet/sum95e.html

1995 Canadian Federal Budget
http://www.fin.gc.ca/budget95/docliste.html

Archives
http://www.fin.gc.ca/arche.html

Information Paper for Consultations on the Canada Pension Plan
http://www.fin.gc.ca/cpp/cpp-e.pdf

HOTLINKS

Banks and Other Financial Institutions
http://www.fin.gc.ca/links/bankse.html

Corporate Finance Institutions
http://www.fin.gc.ca/links/corpfine.html

Economics
http://www.fin.gc.ca/links/econe.html

Government
http://www.fin.gc.ca/links/gove.html

International Trade and Finance
http://www.fin.gc.ca/links/itfe.html

Public Finance
http://www.fin.gc.ca/links/pubfine.html

Department of Justice Canada

http://canada.justice.gc.ca/index_en.html

THE HON. ALLAN ROCK, MINISTER
http://canada.justice.gc.ca/Presentation/A_ROCK/resume_en.html

ABOUT THE DEPARTMENT
http://canada.justice.gc.ca/Presentation/index_en.html

MISSION STATEMENT
http://canada.justice.gc.ca/Presentation/Mission/mission_en.html

DEPARTMENTAL ROLE
http://canada.justice.gc.ca/Presentation/Role/dojrole_en.html

OUR JUSTICE SYSTEM
http://canada.justice.gc.ca/Publications/Info_education/CSJ/index_en.html

OUR COURT SYSTEM
http://canada.justice.gc.ca/Publications/Info_education/CCS/index_en.html

LAWS
http://canada.justice.gc.ca/loireg/index_en.html

BILLS AND STATUTES
http://canada.justice.gc.ca/Projets_loi/index_en.html

CONFERENCES
http://canada.justice.gc.ca/Conferences/index_en.html

PUBLICATIONS
http://canada.justice.gc.ca/Publications/index_en.html

Elections Canada

http://www.elections.ca/

TABLE OF CONTENTS

http://www.elections.ca/index_e.html

ABOUT ELECTIONS CANADA

http://www.elections.ca/basic/index.html

Find press releases, information about elections and by-elections, and . . .

Message from the Chief Electoral Officer

http://www.elections.ca/basic/message.html

Out-of-Town Voting

http://www.elections.ca/basic/away.html

Information for Prospective Candidates

http://www.elections.ca/basic/candidates.html

Electoral System Accessibility

http://www.elections.ca/basic/accessible.html

Canada Elections Act Investigative Process

http://www.elections.ca/basic/investigate.html

RIDING INFORMATION

http://www.elections.ca/specific/index.html

CONTACT INFORMATION

http://www.elections.ca/email.html

Emergency Preparedness Canada

http://hoshi.cic.sfu.ca/epc/

SEND YOUR COMMENTS
Email: cominfo@jackson.epc.epc-pcc.x400.gc.ca

ABOUT EMERGENCY PREPAREDNESS CANADA
http://hoshi.cic.sfu.ca/epc/EPCsum.html

INFORMATION DOCUMENTS
Emergency Preparedness Digest
http://hoshi.cic.sfu.ca/epc/DIGEST/jan96/EPDhome.htm

Preparing for the Woods
http://hoshi.cic.sfu.ca/~safegard/english/publications/woods-e.html

Winter Driving
http://hoshi.cic.sfu.ca/~safegard/english/publications/driving-e.html

Preparing for an Earthquake
http://hoshi.cic.sfu.ca/epc/HIGHRISE/english.html

Emergency Food and Water Pack
http://hoshi.cic.sfu.ca/epc/FOODWATR/english.html

Emergency Preparedness for Seniors
http://hoshi.cic.sfu.ca/epc/SENIORS/english.html

Federal Policy for Emergencies
http://hoshi.cic.sfu.ca/epc/POLICY/english.html

Highlights of the Emergencies Act
http://hoshi.cic.sfu.ca/epc/GENCIES.ACT/english.html

B.C. Earthquake Support
http://hoshi.cic.sfu.ca/epc/NESP/english.html

Disaster Financial Assistance Arrangements
http://hoshi.cic.sfu.ca/epc/DFA/english.html

Videos Available
http://hoshi.cic.sfu.ca/epc/VIDEO/english.html

CONTACTS
http://hoshi.cic.sfu.ca/epc/CONTACTS/english.html

ADDRESSES
http://hoshi.cic.sfu.ca/epc/CEPC/cepc-addresses.html

CANADIAN EMERGENCY PREPAREDNESS COLLEGE, ARNPRIOR, ONTARIO
http://hoshi.cic.sfu.ca/epc/CEPC/cepc.html

About the Courses
http://hoshi.cic.sfu.ca/epc/CEPC/cepc-outline.html

Schedule
http://hoshi.cic.sfu.ca/epc/CEPC/cepc-schedule.html

Environment Canada

http://www.doe.ca/

THE HON. SERGIO MARCHI, MINISTER
http://www.doe.ca/minister/minbio_e.htm

WHAT'S NEW
http://www.doe.ca/wneweng.html

ABOUT THE DEPARTMENT
http://www.doe.ca/who/abouteng.html

RELEVANT ACTS
http://www.doe.ca/who/acteng.html

ENVIRONMENT CANADA PROGRAMS
Atmospheric Environment Program
http://www.doe.ca/who/aese.html

Environmental Protection Program
http://www.doe.ca/who/epse.html

Environmental Conservation Program
http://www.doe.ca/who/ece.html

GREAT LAKES INFORMATION MANAGEMENT RESOURCE
http://www.cciw.ca/glimr/intro.html

DEPARTMENTAL ACTION PLAN
http://www.doe.ca/ecbp/

ISSUES AND TOPICS
(Recent highlights, issues, press releases, speeches, and enforcement action)
http://www.doe.ca/isseng.html

CALENDAR OF CONSULTATIONS
http://www.doe.ca/consult/ecal.htm

PRODUCTS AND SERVICES
http://www.doe.ca/prodeng.html

Inquiries
http://www.doe.ca/prod/inqry-e.html

Library
http://www.doe.ca/library/libhome.html

Library Publications
http://www.doe.ca/library/deptpubs/pubs.html

Web Hotlist of Environment-Related Sites
http://www.doe.ca/library/internet/sites.html

Departmental Publications
http://www.doe.ca/prod/publications-e.html

Wildlife: Hinterland's Who's Who
http://www.doe.ca/envcan/index.html

List of Free Publications
http://www.doe.ca/prod/pop-e.html

Ecocycle
http://www.doe.ca/prod/ecocycle/eecocycl.html

Ice Services
http://www.on.doe.ca/ice/home.ice.html

WEATHER
Forecasts
(With a colourful and clickable map of Canada)
http://www.on.doe.ca/text/index.html

Charts
http://www.on.doe.ca/charts/index.shtml

Maps
http://www.dow.on.doe.ca/maps/index.html

Satellite Images
gopher://www.dow.on.doe.ca/11/photos

INFOBASE ABOUT THE STATE OF CANADA'S ENVIRONMENT
http://199.212.18.12/~soer/

ENVIROFAX
http://www.doe.ca/efaxe.html

ABOUT THE GREEN LANE
http://www.doe.ca/greeneng.html

REGIONAL GREEN LANE SITES
http://www.doe.ca/regeng.html

SEND YOUR COMMENTS
http://www.doe.ca/feedeng.html

Export Development Corporation

http://www.edc.ca/

TABLE OF CONTENTS
http://www.edc.ca/english/index.html

WHAT'S NEW
http://www.edc.ca/english/news/index.html

PRESS RELEASES
http://www.edc.ca/english/news/press/index.html

FREQUENTLY ASKED QUESTIONS
http://www.edc.ca/english/news/FAQ/FAQ.html

ABOUT THE EDC
http://www.edc.ca/english/info/index.html

WHAT IS THE EDC?
http://www.edc.ca/english/info/99-02inf.html

OPERATIONS
http://www.edc.ca/english/info/edctoday/index.html

ANNUAL REPORT
http://www.edc.ca/english/info/anumrprt/index.html

CAREER INFORMATION
http://www.edc.ca/english/info/humres.html

EXPORTING INFORMATION
http://www.edc.ca/english/info/roadmap.html

INFORMATION FOR SMALL BUSINESS
http://www.edc.ca/english/smallbusiness/index.html

Exporting with EDC
http://www.edc.ca/english/smallbusiness/wmbfse.html

Export Credit Insurance
http://www.edc.ca/english/smallbusiness/excreins.html

Lines of Credit
http://www.edc.ca/english/smallbusiness/excreins.html

Domestic Credit Insurance
http://www.edc.ca/english/smallbusiness/domcrins.html

RISK MANAGEMENT
http://www.edc.ca/english/services/index.html

Product Information
http://www.edc.ca/english/services/genprod/index.html

Insurance Products and Services
http://www.edc.ca/english/services/insprod/index.html

Financing Products and Services
http://www.edc.ca/english/services/finprod/index.html

Lines of Credit Around the World
http://www.edc.ca/english/services/finprod/loc-eng.html

Export Financing Guidelines
http://www.edc.ca/english/services/finprod/99-44.html

COUNTRY/MARKET INFORMATION
http://www.edc.ca/english/cm_info/index.html

Export Performance Monitor
http://www.edc.ca/english/cm_info/mon-oct.html

Canadian Export Environment
http://www.edc.ca/english/cm_info/cee.html

Export Market Risk Environment
http://www.edc.ca/english/cm_info/emre.html

HOTLINKS
http://www.edc.ca/english/websites/index.html

CONTACTS
http://www.edc.ca/english/info/contact.html

SEND YOUR COMMENTS
Email:

Marketing
export@edc4.edc.ca

Media
gilero@edc4.edc.ca

Farm Credit Corporation Canada

http://canada.gc.ca/depts/agencies/fccind_e.html

The Farm Credit Corporation provides financing to the farming sector.

This site is not yet fully developed at the time of publication of this book and offers limited information pertaining to the corporation's mandate and field of responsibility.

Federal Office of Regional Development (Quebec)

http://canada.gc.ca/depts/agencies/frqind_e.html

The Federal Office of Regional Development (Quebec) promotes economic development in slow growth areas of the Quebec economy.

This site is not yet fully developed at the time of publication of this book and offers limited information pertaining to the office's mandate and field of responsibility.

Fisheries and Oceans Canada

http://www.ncr.dfo.ca/

WHAT'S NEW
http://www.ncr.dfo.ca/new/new_e.htm

ABOUT DFO
http://www.ncr.dfo.ca/dfo_mpo/dfo_e.htm

ABOUT THE MINISTER
http://www.ncr.dfo.ca/minister/minister.htm

AQUACULTURE
http://www.ncr.dfo.ca/aquacult/aquaforu/aquafo_e.htm

PUBLICATIONS
http://www.ncr.dfo.ca/communic/comm1_e.htm

REGIONS
http://www.ncr.dfo.ca/regions/regions.htm

HOTLINKS
http://www.ncr.dfo.ca/LINKS/HOME_E.HTM

SEND YOUR COMMENTS
http://www.ncr.dfo.ca/MAILTO/mailto.htm

Foreign Affairs and International Trade

http://www.dfait-maeci.gc.ca/

TABLE OF CONTENTS
http://www.dfait-maeci.gc.ca/english/menu.htm

ABOUT THE DEPARTMENT
http://www.dfait-maeci.gc.ca/english/infoweb/menu.htm

Overview
http://www.dfait-maeci.gc.ca/english/html/10/10001.htm

The Ministers
http://www.dfait-maeci.gc.ca/english/infoweb/minister/menu.htm

Lloyd Axworthy
(Minister of Foreign Affairs)
http://www.dfait-maeci.gc.ca/english/infoweb/minister/axwort-e.htm

Art Eggleton
(Minister for International Trade)
http://www.dfait-maeci.gc.ca/english/infoweb/minister/eggle-e.htm

Pierre Pettigrew
(Minister for International Cooperation)
http://www.dfait-maeci.gc.ca/english/infoweb/minister/pettig-e.htm

Christine Stewart
(Secretary of State for Latin America and Africa)
http://www.dfait-maeci.gc.ca/english/infoweb/minister/stewart.htm

Raymond Chan
(Secretary of State for Asia-Pacific)
http://www.dfait-maeci.gc.ca/english/infoweb/minister/chan.htm

Frequently Asked Questions
http://www.dfait-maeci.gc.ca/english/faq/menu.htm

About Emergencies and Disasters Abroad
http://www.dfait-maeci.gc.ca/english/faq/disast-e.htm

About International Trade
http://www.dfait-maeci.gc.ca/english/trade/tradefaq.htm

Guide for International Investors
http://www.dfait-maeci.gc.ca/english/html/60/60020.htm

WHAT'S NEW
http://www.dfait-maeci.gc.ca/english/whatsnew/menu.htm

INFORMATION SOURCES
http://www.dfait-maeci.gc.ca/english/inet/menu.htm

CANADIAN INTERNATIONAL RELATIONS CHRONICLE
http://www.dfait-maeci.gc.ca/english/news/newsletr/chronik/chro1-e1.htm

INFOCENTRE
http://www.dfait-maeci.gc.ca/english/html/05/05005.htm

BULLETIN BOARD
http://www.dfait-maeci.gc.ca/english/html/05/05015.htm

FAXLINK
http://www.dfait-maeci.gc.ca/english/html/05/05010.htm

INTERNATIONAL FAXLINK
http://www.dfait-maeci.gc.ca/english/html/other/ifaxlink.htm

CANADA BUSINESS SERVICE CENTRES
http://www.dfait-maeci.gc.ca/english/html/10/10002.htm

LIBRARY SERVICES
http://www.dfait-maeci.gc.ca/english/inet/librarye.htm

CANADIAN EMBASSIES
http://www.dfait-maeci.gc.ca/english/missions/menu.htm

CANADIAN MISSIONS ABROAD
http://www.dfait-maeci.gc.ca/english/html/60/60001.htm

HONORARY CONSULS ABROAD
http://www.dfait-maeci.gc.ca/english/html/05/05112.htm

INTERNATIONAL TRADE CENTRES IN CANADA
http://www.dfait-maeci.gc.ca/english/html/60/60002.htm

TRADE OFFICES IN OTTAWA
http://www.dfait-maeci.gc.ca/english/html/05/05103.htm

FOREIGN EMBASSIES IN CANADA
http://www.ncf.carleton.ca/freeport/government/embassies/menu

Europe
http://www.ncf.carleton.ca/freeport/government/embassies/europe/menu

Middle East
http://www.ncf.carleton.ca/freeport/government/embassies/mid.east/menu

Asia
http://www.ncf.carleton.ca/freeport/government/embassies/asia/menu

North America
http://www.ncf.carleton.ca/freeport/government/embassies/north.am/menu

South America
http://www.ncf.carleton.ca/freeport/government/embassies/south.am/menu

Africa
http://www.ncf.carleton.ca/freeport/government/embassies/africa/menu

DIRECTORY OF DIPLOMATIC REPRESENTATIVES IN CANADA
http://www.arraydev.com/commerce/emb-bck.html

INFORMATION BY SUBJECT
http://www.dfait-maeci.gc.ca/english/menu2.htm

Foreign Affairs
http://www.dfait-maeci.gc.ca/english/foreignp/menu.htm

International Trade
http://www.dfait-maeci.gc.ca/english/trade/menu.htm

NORTH AMERICAN FREE TRADE AGREEMENT (NAFTA)
http://www.dfait-maeci.gc.ca/english/html/51/51001.htm

INTERNATIONAL CULTURAL RELATIONS
http://www.dfait-maeci.gc.ca/english/culture/menu.htm

GUIDE FOR CANADIAN PERFORMING ARTISTS ENTERING U.S. (VISAS)
http://www.dfait-maeci.gc.ca/english/culture/guidecul/guidarti.htm

RESIDENCIES IN MEXICO AND U.S.
http://www.dfait-maeci.gc.ca/english/culture/residenc.htm

ARTS AND LETTERS
http://www.dfait-maeci.gc.ca/english/culture/perform/perform.htm

VISUAL ARTS
http://www.dfait-maeci.gc.ca/english/culture/visual.htm

LITERATURE
http://www.dfait-maeci.gc.ca/english/culture/literatu.htm

PUBLISHING
http://www.dfait-maeci.gc.ca/english/culture/publish.htm

FILM, VIDEO, AND SOUND RECORDING
http://www.dfait-maeci.gc.ca/english/culture/film.htm

CANADIAN ACADEMIC AND CULTURAL REPRESENTATIVES — POSTINGS ABROAD
http://www.dfait-maeci.gc.ca/english/html/culture/canreps.htm

CANADIAN ACADEMIC AND CULTURAL REPRESENTATIVES IN CANADA
http://www.dfait-maeci.gc.ca/english/culture/hqcontac.htm

CANADIAN STUDIES PROGRAM
http://www.dfait-maeci.gc.ca/english/html/culture/canstud.htm

INTERNATIONAL YOUTH EXCHANGE
http://www.dfait-maeci.gc.ca/english/html/culture/youthex.htm

CONSULAR SERVICES
http://www.dfait-maeci.gc.ca/english/consular/menu.htm

BEFORE YOUR TRIP
http://www.dfait-maeci.gc.ca/english/consular/bvbe.htm

ASSISTANCE FOR CANADIANS OVERSEAS
http://www.dfait-maeci.gc.ca/english/consular/web.htm

DETENTION OR IMPRISONMENT ABROAD:
A GUIDE TO CANADIAN CONSULAR SERVICES
http://www.dfait-maeci.gc.ca/english/consular/candetai.htm

PASSPORT OFFICE
http://www.ncf.carleton.ca/freeport/government/federal/passport/menu

INFORMATION BY REGION AND COUNTRY
http://www.dfait-maeci.gc.ca/english/geo/menu.htm

United States
http://www.dfait-maeci.gc.ca/english/geo/m51.htm

Asia-Pacific
http://www.dfait-maeci.gc.ca/english/geo/m52.htm

Latin America and Caribbean
http://www.dfait-maeci.gc.ca/english/geo/m53.htm

Western Europe and European Union
http://www.dfait-maeci.gc.ca/english/geo/m54.htm

Eastern Europe and Commonwealth of Independent States
http://www.dfait-maeci.gc.ca/english/geo/m55.htm

Africa and Middle East
http://www.dfait-maeci.gc.ca/english/geo/m56.htm

BUSINESS TRIPS TO CANADA — USEFUL TIPS
http://www.dfait-maeci.gc.ca/english/html/60/60050.htm

This site provides helpful information about entrance requirements and customs, climate, time zones, Daylight Saving Time, business hours, currency, language, accommodation, electric current, laundry and dry cleaning, telegrams, tipping, transportation, shopping, holidays, and cuisine.

NEWS RELEASES, STATEMENTS, AND NEWSLETTERS
http://www.dfait-maeci.gc.ca/english/news/menu.htm

GOPHER SITE
http://www.dfait-maeci.gc.ca/english/docs/menu.htm

Freshwater Fish Marketing Corporation

http://canada.gc.ca/depts/agencies/fwfind_e.html

The Freshwater Fish Marketing Corporation pertains to interprovincial and export trade in freshwater fisheries.

This site is not yet fully developed at the time of publication of this book and offers limited information pertaining to the corporation's mandate and field of responsibility.

Great Lakes Pilotage Authority Canada

http://canada.gc.ca/depts/agencies/glpind_e.html

This Crown corporation is one of four pilotage authorities in Canada.

This site is not yet fully developed at the time of publication of this book and offers limited information pertaining to the authority's mandate and field of responsibility.

Hazardous Materials Information Review Commission

http://canada.gc.ca/depts/agencies/hmiind_e.html

This site is not yet fully developed at the time of publication of this book and offers limited information pertaining to the commission's mandate and field of responsibility.

Health Canada

http://www.hwc.ca/

SEND YOUR COMMENTS
http://www.hwc.ca/links/forms/comments.html

WHAT'S NEW
http://www.hwc.ca/links/whatne_e.htm

TABLE OF CONTENTS
http://www.hwc.ca/links/english.html

ABOUT THE DEPARTMENT
http://www.hwc.ca/links/healthcan/abthc_e.htm

ABOUT THE MINISTER
http://www.hwc.ca/datapcb/communc/home/minbioe.htm

FINDING HEALTH INFORMATION
http://www.hwc.ca/links/healthcan/hinfo_e.htm

Web Search Engine
http://www.hwc.ca/cgi-bin/hcsearch.pl

Gopher
gopher://hpb1.hwc.ca/

ftp
ftp://hpb1.hwc.ca/

Communications
http://www.hwc.ca/datapcb/communc/home/english.htm

News Releases
http://www.hwc.ca/datapcb/communc/home/news/titles.htm

Minister's Speeches
http://www.hwc.ca/datapcb/communc/home/speeches/titles.htm

Departmental Publications
(Topics include AIDS, alcohol, family violence, seniors, nutrition, etc.)
http://www.hwc.ca/datapcb/communc/home/pubs/catalogu.htm

Canada Volunteer Award
http://www.hwc.ca/datapcb/communc/home/cva/cvae.htm

About Your Health
(Topics include acne medications, AIDS in food-processing establishments, aluminum in drinking water, bacteria in raw food, barbecue syndrome, breast implants, caffeine, condoms, drinking water guidelines, cookware safety, hepatitis B, meningococcal disease in Canada, menstrual tampons and toxic shock syndrome, cosmetic labelling, and much more.)
http://www.hwc.ca/datapcb/communc/home/issues/titlese.htm

Intracom — Health Canada's Employee Newsletter
http://www.hwc.ca/datapcb/communc/home/english.htm

How to Reach Them
http://www.hwc.ca/datapcb/communc/home/inquiry/inquiry.htm

Library
Telnet: 198.53.18.21; login: hc1; userid: client (no password required)

Health Protection Branch

Policies
http://www.hwc.ca/datahpb/policy/poltab.html

Alerts
http://www.hwc.ca:8400/news/alerts.htm

BBS
Telnet 204.187.49.2 Login: hpbnet

Laboratories
http://www.cisti.nrc.ca/programs/indcan/fedlabs/hc.html

Laboratory Centre for Disease Control
http://www.cisti.nrc.ca/programs/indcan/fedlabs/text/145.html

Environmental Health Directorate
http://www.hwc.ca/datahpb/dataehd/index.html

Pest Management Regulatory Agency
http://www.hwc.ca/datahpb/datapest/index.html

Food Directorate
http://www.hwc.ca/datahpb/datafood/english/welcome.html

Online Health Promotion
http://www.hwc.ca/links/healthcan/hpon_e.htm

Children's Mental Health
http://www.hwc.ca/datahpsb/cmhu/cmhuhome.htm

Women's Health
http://www.hwc.ca/datapcb/datawhb/index.htm

Health Systems and Policy
http://www.hwc.ca/datapcb/datahesa/hex.htm

International Affairs Directorate
http://www.hwc.ca/datapcb/iad/iadtitle.htm

Statistics
http://www.ccsa.ca/stats.htm

National Health Research and Development Program
http://www.hwc.ca/datahpsb/nhrdp/index.html

Health Promotion and Programs Branch
Systems for Health Directorate
http://www.hwc.ca/datahpsb/hssd/intqual.htm

Nutrition Programs Unit
http://www.hwc.ca/datahpsb/npu/index.html

Seniors Directorate
http://www.hwc.ca/datahpsb/seniors/senpage.html

STANDING COMMITTEE ON HEALTH
http://www.parl.gc.ca/cgi-bin/committees/english_committee.pl?sant

STANDING COMMITTEE ON HIV/AIDS
http://www.parl.gc.ca/cgi-bin/committees/english_committee.pl?shiv

NATIONAL FORUM ON HEALTH
http://www.hwc.ca:8200/

ALPHABETICAL LISTING OF HEALTH TOPICS
http://www.hwc.ca/links/htopic/topic_e.htm

HEALTH RESOURCE FUNDING
http://www.hwc.ca/links/hother/funding.htm

LINKS
Health Canada Partners
http://www.hwc.ca/links/hother/hpart_e.htm

Canadian Health-Related Groups
http://www.hwc.ca/links/hother/cdnhea_e.htm

International Health-Related Sites
http://www.hwc.ca/links/hother/intern_e.htm

Science Sites
http://www.hwc.ca/links/hscience/scienc_e.htm

Other Health Resource Links
http://www.hwc.ca/links/hmisc/misc_e.htm
and
http://www.hwc.ca/links/hother/healis_e.htm

POST HEALTH NOTICES
http://www.hwc.ca/webboard/index.html

POST TO THE EVENTS CALENDAR
http://www.hwc.ca/cgi-bin/people/tmoorby/WebEvent/WebEvent

JOIN HEALTH WEBCHAT
http://www.hwc.ca/webchat/chat.html

JOIN HEALTH INTERNET RELAY CHAT
http://www.hwc.ca/wwwirc/wwwirc.html

DEPARTMENTAL ASSISTANCE ABOUT EMAIL
http://www.hwc.ca/links/tech/email/emailint.html

Human Resources Development Canada

http://www.hrdc-drhc.gc.ca/

TABLE OF CONTENTS
http://www.hrdc-drhc.gc.ca/hrdc/menu-en.html

WHAT'S NEW
http://www.hrdc-drhc.gc.ca/hrdc/common/whatnew.html

PRESS RELEASES
http://www.hrdc-drhc.gc.ca/hrdc/common/press_e.html

ABOUT THE DEPARTMENT
http://www.hrdc-drhc.gc.ca/hrdc/dept/depind_e.html

DEPARTMENTAL INITIATIVES
http://www.hrdc-drhc.gc.ca/hrdc/initiatv/intind_e.html

Social Security Reform
http://www.hrdc-drhc.gc.ca/hrdc/essrpage.html

PROGRAMS AND SERVICES
Income Security Programs

Overview
http://www.hrdc-drhc.gc.ca/hrdc/isp/ispove_e.html

Old Age Security
http://www.hrdc-drhc.gc.ca/hrdc/isp/oas/oasind_e.html

Current Old Age Security Payment Rates
http://www.hrdc-drhc.gc.ca/hrdc/isp/oas/rates_e.html

Canada Student Loans Program
http://www.hrdc-drhc.gc.ca/hrdc/hrib/learnlit/ops/slpind_e.html

Canada Pension Plan
http://www.hrdc-drhc.gc.ca/hrdc/isp/cpp/cppind_e.html

Overview
http://www.hrdc-drhc.gc.ca/hrdc/isp/cpp/cppove_e.html

Retirement Pension
http://www.hrdc-drhc.gc.ca/hrdc/isp/cpp/retire_e.html

Disability Benefits
http://www.hrdc-drhc.gc.ca/hrdc/isp/cpp/disabi_e.html

Survivor Benefits
http://www.hrdc-drhc.gc.ca/hrdc/isp/cpp/surviv_e.html

Credit Splitting
http://www.hrdc-drhc.gc.ca/hrdc/isp/cpp/credit_e.html

Acts and Regulations
(Old Age Security Act and Canada Pension Act)
http://www.hrdc-drhc.gc.ca/hrdc/isp/acts_e.html

News Releases
http://www.hrdc-drhc.gc.ca/hrdc/isp/newsrele/newind_e.html

Current CPP Payment Rates
http://www.hrdc-drhc.gc.ca/hrdc/isp/cpp/rates_e.html

Frequently Asked Questions (FAQ)
http://www.hrdc-drhc.gc.ca/hrdc/isp/cpp/genera_e.html

International Agreements
http://www.hrdc-drhc.gc.ca/hrdc/isp/internat/intind_e.html

Improving Service
http://www.hrdc-drhc.gc.ca/hrdc/isp/improv/impro_e.html

Community Partnerships
http://www.hrdc-drhc.gc.ca/hrdc/isp/partners/cppout_e.html

Publications
http://www.hrdc-drhc.gc.ca/hrdc/isp/pubind_e.html

Labour
http://www.hrdc-drhc.gc.ca/hrdc/labour/index.html

Press Releases
http://www.hrdc-drhc.gc.ca/hrdc/labour/newind_e.html

About the Canada Labour Code
http://www.hrdc-drhc.gc.ca/hrdc/labour/labstand/index.html

Workplace Information
http://www.hrdc-drhc.gc.ca/hrdc/bli/eng/bli.html

Youth
Youth Internship in Canada
http://www.hrdc-drhc.gc.ca/hrdc/youth/mrcnr-e.html

Youth Service in Canada
http://www.hrdc-drhc.gc.ca/hrdc/ysc/yschomee.html

CORPORATE SERVICES
Program Evaluation
http://www.hrdc-drhc.gc.ca/hrdc/corp/stratpol/progeval/proind_e.html

About Program Evaluation
http://www.hrdc-drhc.gc.ca/hrdc/corp/stratpol/progeval/intro_e.html

Library
http://www.hrdc-drhc.gc.ca/hrdc/library/libe.html

Subject List
http://www.hrdc-drhc.gc.ca/hrdc/library/subje.html

Contact Information
http://www.hrdc-drhc.gc.ca/hrdc/library/visite.html

Using Primo Online Catalog
http://www.hrdc-drhc.gc.ca/hrdc/library/primoe.html

GETTING CANADIANS BACK TO WORK
http://www.hrdc-drhc.gc.ca/hrdc/initiatv/eilaunch/propos_e.html

CANADIAN WORKPLACE RESEARCH NETWORK (CWRN)
http://www.hrdc-drhc.gc.ca/hrdc/labour/fedmed/cwrnet/cwrind_e.html

PARTNERSHIP LINKS
http://www.hrdc-drhc.gc.ca/hrdc/partner/prtind_e.html

LINKS TO OTHER HDRC OFFICES
http://www.hrdc-drhc.gc.ca/hrdc/other/other_e.html

SEND YOUR COMMENTS
Email: douglas.young@hrdc-drhc.gc.ca

Immigration and Refugee Board

http://www.ncf.carleton.ca/freeport/government/federal/irb/menu

ABOUT THE BOARD
http://www.ncf.carleton.ca/freenet/rootdir/menus/government/federal/irb/whatis

CONVENTION REFUGEE DETERMINATION DIVISION
http://www.ncf.carleton.ca/freenet/rootdir/menus/government/federal/irb/crdd.eng

IMMIGRATION APPEAL DIVISION
http://www.ncf.carleton.ca/freenet/rootdir/menus/government/federal/irb/iad.eng

ADJUDICATION DIVISION
http://www.ncf.carleton.ca/freenet/rootdir/menus/government/federal/irb/adj.eng

1994 ANNUAL REPORT
http://www.ncf.carleton.ca/freenet/rootdir/menus/government/federal/irb/1994.eng

Indian and Northern Affairs Canada

http://www.inac.gc.ca/

THE HON. RON IRWIN, MINISTER
http://www.inac.gc.ca/info/minister.html

Also contains information about the DM and ADM.

PREVIOUS MINISTERS
(1755 to 1994)
http://www.inac.gc.ca/pubs/information/info38.html

PRESS RELEASES
http://www.inac.gc.ca/news/index.html

TABLE OF CONTENTS
http://www.inac.gc.ca/index_e.html

ABOUT THE DEPARTMENT
http://www.inac.gc.ca/info/index.html
and
http://www.inac.gc.ca/pubs/information/info15.html

MISSION STATEMENT
http://www.inac.gc.ca/info/mission.html

HISTORY OF THE DEPARTMENT
http://www.inac.gc.ca/info/history.html

CONTACT LIST
http://www.inac.gc.ca/info/contact.html

PUBLICATIONS
http://www.inac.gc.ca/pubs/index.html

The Canadian Indian
http://www.inac.gc.ca/pubs/indian/

Inuit Sculpture
http://www.inac.gc.ca/pubs/sculpture/

INFORMATION SITE
http://www.inac.gc.ca/pubs/information/

About Aboriginal Land Claims in Canada
http://www.inac.gc.ca/pubs/information/info01.html

About Aboriginal Self-Government
http://www.inac.gc.ca/pubs/information/info03.html

Bill C-31
http://www.inac.gc.ca/pubs/information/info02.html

Tungavik Federation of Nunavut (TFN)
http://www.inac.gc.ca/pubs/information/info08.html

Comprehensive Claims
http://www.inac.gc.ca/pubs/information/info09.html

Dene/Métis Comprehensive Claim Chronology
http://www.inac.gc.ca/pubs/information/info10.html

The Cree-Naskapi (of Quebec) Act
http://www.inac.gc.ca/pubs/information/info11.html

The James Bay and Northern Quebec Agreement and the Northeastern Quebec Agreement
http://www.inac.gc.ca/pubs/information/info14.html

Labrador Inuit Association Comprehensive Land Claim
http://www.inac.gc.ca/pubs/information/info17.html

Council of Yukon First Nations Comprehensive Land Claim
http://www.inac.gc.ca/pubs/information/info18.html

Self-Government Sechelt Style
http://www.inac.gc.ca/pubs/information/info20.html

The Gwich'in (Dene/Métis) Comprehensive Land Claim Agreement
http://www.inac.gc.ca/pubs/information/info22.html

Band Support Funding
http://www.inac.gc.ca/pubs/information/info24.html

Nisga'a Treaty Negotiations
http://www.inac.gc.ca/pubs/information/info31.html

Treaty Negotiations in British Columbia
http://www.inac.gc.ca/pubs/information/info36.html

Gitksan-Wet'Suwet'En Tribal Council Comprehensive Land Claim
http://www.inac.gc.ca/pubs/information/info39.html

Indian and Inuit Post-Secondary Education
http://www.inac.gc.ca/pubs/information/info41.html

The Indian Register
http://www.inac.gc.ca/pubs/information/info44.html

Aboriginal Forestry
http://www.inac.gc.ca/pubs/information/info45.html

Indian Residential Schools
http://www.inac.gc.ca/pubs/information/info46.html

Band Property Taxation Powers on Reserves
http://www.inac.gc.ca/pubs/information/info51.html

The Algonquins of Golden Lake Land Claim
http://www.inac.gc.ca/pubs/information/info52.html

Territory of Nunavut
http://www.inac.gc.ca/pubs/information/info55.html

Wahta Mohawks (Gibson) Specific Claim
http://www.inac.gc.ca/pubs/information/info61.html

The Innu of Newfoundland and Labrador
http://www.inac.gc.ca/pubs/information/info62.html

The Lubicon Lake Claim
http://www.inac.gc.ca/pubs/information/info63.html

Progress on Commitments to Aboriginal Peoples
http://www.inac.gc.ca/pubs/information/info69.html

The Arctic Environmental Strategy
http://www.inac.gc.ca/pubs/information/info72.html

Davis Inlet
http://www.inac.gc.ca/pubs/information/davis.html

THE NORTHERN INFORMATION NETWORK
About the NINBBS
http://www.inac.gc.ca/nin/nin.html

Accessing the NINBBS
Telnet: nin.inac.gc.ca; login: nin

FREQUENTLY ASKED QUESTIONS
http://www.inac.gc.ca/faqs/index.html

INDIANS IN CANADA AND THE UNITED STATES
http://www.inac.gc.ca/pubs/information/info37.html

DIRECTORY OF INDIAN AND NATIVE ASSOCIATIONS
http://www.inac.gc.ca/pubs/indian/org.html

RELATED SITES
http://www.inac.gc.ca/sites/index.html

Aboriginal Youth Network
http://ayn.ca/

Arctic Information Sources
http://www.ucalgary.ca/~tull/arctic/

Maps of Canada-Indian Treaties
http://ellesmere.ccm.emr.ca/wwwnais/select/indian/english/html/indian.html

Native American Resources on the Net
http://hanksville.phast.umass.edu/misc/NAresources.html

NativeWeb
http://web.maxwell.syr.edu/nativeweb

Nunavut Planning Commission
http://npc.nunavut.ca/

Aboriginal Enterprise
http://flocon.vli.ca/spirit

Fourth World Documentation Project:
http://www.halcyon.com/FWDP/fwdp.html

SEND YOUR COMMENTS
Email: chodae@inac.gc.ca

Industry Canada

http://info.ic.gc.ca/ic-data/ic-eng.html

THE HON. JOHN MANLEY, MINISTER
http://info.ic.gc.ca/ic-data/general/manley.html
Email: manley.john@ic.gc.ca

THE HON. JOHN GERARD, SECRETARY OF STATE
(Science, Research and Development)
http://info.ic.gc.ca/ic-data/general/gerrard.html
Email: gerrard.jon@ic.gc.ca

WHAT'S NEW
http://info.ic.gc.ca/ic-data/announcements/announce-e.html

SEARCH
http://info.ic.gc.ca/ic-data/ghindex.html

ABOUT THE DEPARTMENT
http://info.ic.gc.ca/ic-data/general/general-e.html

MISSION STATEMENT
http://info.ic.gc.ca/ic-data/general/mission-e.html

LINES OF BUSINESS
http://info.ic.gc.ca/ic-data/general/lines-e.html

TELEPHONE LIST
http://info.ic.gc.ca/ic-data/general/contact/contact.e.html

COMPUTERS FOR SCHOOLS PROGRAM
http://info.ic.gc.ca/ic-data/cfs/index.html

STRATEGIS — BUSINESS INFORMATION SITE
http://strategis.ic.gc.ca

ECONOMY AND TRADE
http://info.ic.gc.ca/ic-data/economy/economy-e.html

INDUSTRY SECTOR
http://info.ic.gc.ca/ic-data/industry/industry-e.html

Forest Industries and Building Products
http://info.ic.gc.ca/ic-data/industry/forestind/english/home.html

Industry Sector Profiles
gopher://info.ic.gc.ca:70/11/ic-data/industry/Industry.Profiles/

Information Technologies

Doing Business in China
http://info.ic.gc.ca/ic-data/industry/china/eng/indexe.html

Information Technology and Productivity in the Canadian Economy
http://info.ic.gc.ca/ic-data/industry/info.tech.e.txt

Tourism

Canadian Tourism Commission
http://info.ic.gc.ca/ic-data/industry/tourism/index-e.html

Information Highway
http://info.ic.gc.ca/ic-data/info-highway/ih-e.html

Information Highway Advisory Council
http://info.ic.gc.ca/info-highway/ih.html
Email: council@ic.gc.ca

Community Access Program
http://cnet.unb.ca/cap/

Marketplace Rules and Services
Links to Information Pertaining to:
Competition Bureau
Canadian Intellectual Property Office (CIPO)
Corporate Governance Branch
http://info.ic.gc.ca/ic-data/marketplace/market-e.html

Ethics Counsellor
Lobbyists' Code of Conduct Discussion Paper
http://info.ic.gc.ca/ic-data/marketplace/ethics/l_code_e.html

Lobbyists Registration Act (Annual Report)
http://info.ic.gc.ca/ic-data/marketplace/ethics/lobbyists.1995.e.html

SCIENCE AND TECHNOLOGY
http://info.ic.gc.ca/ic-data/science/science-e.html

Education
Canada's SchoolNet
http://schoolnet2.carleton.ca/

National Atlas on SchoolNet
http://www-nais.ccm.emr.ca/schoolnet/

Research Institutions
Centre for Information Technology Innovation (CITI)
http://www.citi.doc.ca

Communications Research Centre (CRC)
http://www.crc.doc.ca/index.html

Directory of Federal Laboratories
http://www.cisti.nrc.ca/programs/indcan/fedlabs/homepage.html

Other Science and Technology Sites
Canadian Technology Gateway
http://www.cisti.nrc.ca/programs/indcan/ctg.html

Canadian Technology Network
http://ctn.nrc.ca

National Advisory Board on Science and Technology
http://info.ic.gc.ca/opengov/nabst/nabst.html

SMALL BUSINESS
http://info.ic.gc.ca/ic-data/sm-business/sm-bus-e.html

ABORIGINAL BUSINESS CANADA
http://www.vli.ca/clients/abc/abenaki/abcmain.htm

TELECOMMUNICATIONS
http://info.ic.gc.ca/ic-data/telecom/telecom-e.html

Canada Gazette
http://info.ic.gc.ca/ic-data/telecom/gazette/gazette-e.html

Canada Gazette Email List
http://info.ic.gc.ca/ic-data/telecom/gazette/subscribe-e.html

Radiocommunication Act/Telecommunications Act Notices
http://info.ic.gc.ca/ic-data/telecom/gazette/dgtp-e.html

Spectrum Engineering Branch
http://info.ic.gc.ca/ic-data/telecom/dgse/index.html

Emergency Telecommunications Branch
http://hoshi.cic.sfu.ca/ic/

INDUSTRY-RELATED LINKS
http://info.ic.gc.ca/ic-data/general/links-e.html

SEND YOUR COMMENTS
http://info.ic.gc.ca/ic-data/comments-e.html

Institute for Marine Dynamics

http://www.corpserv.nrc.ca/corpserv/imd.html

RESEARCH PROGRAMS
http://www.corpserv.nrc.ca/corpserv/prog_e.html

FACILITIES
http://www.corpserv.nrc.ca/corpserv/faci_e.html

KEY PERSONNEL
http://www.corpserv.nrc.ca/corpserv/pers_e.html

THE IMD NEWS PUBLICATION
http://www.corpserv.nrc.ca/corpserv/news_e.html

SEND YOUR COMMENTS
Email: nmurphy@minnie.imd.nrc.ca

Intergovernmental Affairs

http://www.aia.gc.ca/

MESSAGE FROM THE MINISTER
http://www.aia.gc.ca/welcome/welc_e.html

ABOUT THE MINISTER
http://www.aia.gc.ca/bio/bio_e.html

SPEECHES
http://www.aia.gc.ca/speeches/speech_e.html

NEWS RELEASES
http://www.aia.gc.ca/news/news_e.html

SEND YOUR COMMENTS
http://www.aia.gc.ca/comments/cmt_e.html

International Development Research Centre

http://www.idrc.ca/

BOARD OF GOVERNORS
http://www.idrc.ca/corp/ebog.html

HISTORY
http://www.idrc.ca/corp/ehistory.html

NEWS AND EVENTS
http://www.idrc.ca/corp/eevents.html

CONTACT INFORMATION
(Email and postal addresses, telephone and fax numbers)
http://www.idrc.ca/corp/eaddress.html

RESEARCH PROGRAMS
http://www.idrc.ca/corp/eprogram.html

INTERNATIONAL SECRETARIATS
http://www.idrc.ca/corp/eprogram.html#secretariats

TRAINING AND AWARDS
http://www.idrc.ca/awards/index.html

ONLINE PUBLICATIONS

IDRC Books
http://www.idrc.ca/books/index.html

IDRC Reports Magazine
http://www.idrc.ca/books/reports/index.html

Annual Reports
http://www.idrc.ca/corp/annuale.html

RESEARCH RESOURCES

Library
http://www.idrc.ca/library/library.html

BBS
http://www.idrc.ca/library/ddbs/ddbse.html

Documents, Speeches, and Proceedings
http://www.idrc.ca/library/document/document.html

Internet Resources
http://www.idrc.ca/library/world/world.html

Proposal Guidelines
http://www.idrc.ca/corp/idrc.html

Laurentian Pilotage Authority Canada

http://canada.gc.ca/depts/agencies/lpaind_e.html

This Crown corporation is one of four pilotage authorities in Canada. The head office is in Montreal.

This site is not yet fully developed at the time of publication of this book and offers limited information pertaining to the authority's mandate and field of responsibility.

Medical Research Council of Canada

http://www.hwc.ca:8100/mrc.html

ABOUT THE MRC
http://www.hwc.ca:8100/whatis/foldeng.html

TABLE OF CONTENTS
http://www.hwc.ca:8100/title.html

SEARCH ENGINE
http://www.hwc.ca:8100/cgi-bin/mrcsearch.pl

NEWS RELEASES
http://www.hwc.ca:8100/newsrel/96/prtoc.html

MRC COMMUNIQUE
http://www.hwc.ca:8100/communik/toctoc.html

GRANTS AND AWARDS GUIDE
http://www.hwc.ca:8100/gag/9596/gagtoc.html

COMPETITION RESULTS
http://www.hwc.ca:8100/misc/competi.html

EMPLOYMENT OPPORTUNITIES
http://www.hwc.ca:8100/job/jobs.html

MRC DECISIONS
http://www.hwc.ca:8100/decisions/dectoc.html

NETWORKS OF CENTRES OF EXCELLENCE
http://www.hwc.ca:8100/nce/nceeng.html

UNIVERSITY–INDUSTRY PROGRAM
http://www.hwc.ca:8100/ui/ui.html

MRC TELEPHONE AND EMAIL DIRECTORY
http://www.hwc.ca:8100/directory.html

BURROUGHS WELCOME FUND
http://www.hwc.ca:8100/misc/burrough.html

National Archives of Canada

http://www.archives.ca/

ABOUT NATIONAL ARCHIVES
http://www.archives.ca/www/About.html

Introduction
http://www.archives.ca/www/memories.html

The National Archivist
http://www.archives.ca/www/Message.html

Using the Archives
http://www.archives.ca/www/using.html

Management of Government Records
http://www.archives.ca/www/mgr.html

> **Information Standards and Practices**
> (Mandate and functions)
> http://www.archives.ca/www/imsp_mandate.html

Archives Preservation
http://www.archives.ca/www/Preservation.html

Archives Accommodation
(Information about Gatineau, Quebec facility)
http://www.archives.ca/www/Accommodation.html

Links to Other Archival Organizations
http://www.archives.ca/www/OtherArchivalOrgs.html

CANADA'S FLAG DAY
http://www.archives.ca/www/ex/flag/new.htm

GENEALOGY RESEARCH
http://www.archives.ca/www/Genealogy.html

MILITARY AND CIVILIAN PERSONNEL RECORDS
http://www.archives.ca/www/PersonnelRecords.html

HISTORICAL RECORDS OF THE GOVERNMENT OF CANADA
http://www.archives.ca/www/atip.html

OBTAINING COPIES OR REPRODUCTIONS
http://www.archives.ca/www/Reproductions.html

BORROWING MICROFILM
http://www.archives.ca/www/iil.html

DECENTRALIZED ACCESS SITES
http://www.archives.ca/www/AccessSites.html

BOUTIQUE
http://www.archives.ca/www/Boutique.html

EXHIBITIONS
http://www.archives.ca/www/Exhibitions.html

OTHER LINKS
http://www.archives.ca/www/Research.html

CONTACTING THE NATIONAL ARCHIVES
http://www.archives.ca/www/ContactingUs.html

National Arts Centre

http://canada.gc.ca/depts/agencies/nacind_e.html

The National Arts Centre is located in Ottawa and is the country's prime artistic stage.

This site is not yet fully developed at the time of publication of this book and offers limited information pertaining to the centre's mandate and field of responsibility.

National Capital Commission

http://canada.gc.ca/depts/agencies/nccind_e.html

The National Capital Commission works for the betterment of the National Capital region in its capacity as the seat of the Government of Canada.

This site is not yet fully developed at the time of publication of this book and offers limited information pertaining to the commission's mandate and field of responsibility.

National Defence

http://www.dnd.ca/

THE HON. DAVID COLLENETTE, MINISTER
http://www.dnd.ca/MNDBio.html

PRESS RELEASES
http://www.dnd.ca/dinfo/dgpa/news_releases/

TABLE OF CONTENTS
http://www.dnd.ca/dnd.htm

DEPARTMENTAL RE-ENGINEERING INITIATIVE
http://www.dnd.ca/mccrt/index_e.htm

Vision 97
http://www.dnd.ca/mccrt/bdy536.htm

Fact Sheet
http://www.dnd.ca/mccrt/bdy532.htm

Backgrounder
http://www.dnd.ca/mccrt/bdy531.htm

Who's Who
http://www.dnd.ca/mccrt/bdy533.htm

Project Team
http://www.dnd.ca/mccrt/bdy534.htm

DEPARTMENTAL INFORMATION
Policy and Communications
(Public affairs)
http://www.dnd.ca/admpol/index_e.htm

Media Advisories
http://www.dnd.ca/admpol/index_e.htm

White Paper '94
http://www.dnd.ca/dinfo/dgpa/white_paper_94/

Budget
http://www.dnd.ca/dinfo/dgpa/budget96/

Peacekeeping Speakers Bureau
http://www.dnd.ca/dinfo/dgpa/misc/PkSpBurE.html

Material
http://www.dnd.ca/admmat/index_e.htm

Continuous Acquisition and Lifecycle Support
http://cals.debbs.ndhq.dnd.ca/

About CALS
http://cals.debbs.ndhq.dnd.ca/english/general.html

What's New
http://cals.debbs.ndhq.dnd.ca/english/whatsnew.html

CALS Information Kits
http://cals.debbs.ndhq.dnd.ca/english/cals_kits.html

Quality Engineering Test Establishment
http://www.dnd.ca/admmat/qete/qete.htm

About QETE
http://www.dnd.ca/admmat/qete/qete2.htm

Telephone List
http://www.dnd.ca/admmat/qete/phone.htm

Scientific Information Services
http://www.dsis.dnd.ca/

Defence Information Services Organization
http://www.dnd.ca/admdis/disoeng.htm

Inquiries
Email: aa229@issc.debbs.ndhq.dnd.ca

DGIMD

Information Management Planning Framework
http://www.dnd.ca/admdis/dimppc/implan_e/planeng.htm

DIMPPC Email Address List
http://www.dnd.ca/admdis/dimppc/email_en.htm

Reorganization
http://www.dnd.ca/admdis/infomt1e/infomt1e.htm

The DISO Badge
http://www.dnd.ca/admdis/aboutcre/abouteng.htm

Professional Associations
http://www.dnd.ca/admdis/links/english/passoc_e.htm

Standards
http://www.dnd.ca/admdis/links/english/stand_e.htm

PUBLICATIONS
http://www.dnd.ca/admdis/links/english/pubs_e.htm

CANADIAN AIR FORCE
http://www.achq.dnd.ca/

Senior Staff Biographies
http://www.achq.dnd.ca/bios/index.htm

The "Flight Plan"
http://www.achq.dnd.ca/fp97/index.htm

Air Transport Group
http://www.achq.dnd.ca/atg/index.htm

About ATG
http://www.achq.dnd.ca/atg/index.htm

Responsibilities
http://www.achq.dnd.ca/atg/movement.htm

Rescue Coordination Centres (RCC)
http://www.achq.dnd.ca/atg/rcc.htm

Canadian Mission Control Centre
http://www.achq.dnd.ca/atg/cmcc.htm

Search and Rescue Technicians
http://www.achq.dnd.ca/atg/sartech.htm

Major Air Disaster (MAJAID) Kit
http://www.achq.dnd.ca/atg/majaid.htm

Equipment

CC-144 Challenger
http://www.achq.dnd.ca/atg/cc_144.htm

CC-138 (DHC-6) Twin Otter
http://www.achq.dnd.ca/atg/cc_138.htm

CH-113 Labrador Helicopter
http://www.achq.dnd.ca/atg/ch_113.htm

CC-115 (DHC-5) Buffalo
http://www.achq.dnd.ca/atg/cc_115.htm

CC-130 Hercules
http://www.achq.dnd.ca/atg/cc_130.htm

CC-150 Polaris-Airbus A310
http://www.achq.dnd.ca/atg/cc_150.htm

CC-137 Boeing 707
http://www.achq.dnd.ca/atg/cc_137.htm

Roundel Air Force Magazine Online
http://www.achq.dnd.ca/roundel/index.htm

Online Photo Archive
http://www.achq.dnd.ca/archive/index.htm

Air Shows

North American Military Aerobatic Team Schedule
http://www.achq.dnd.ca/airshows/index.htm

Canadian Forces Skyhawks Parachute Team Schedule
http://www.achq.dnd.ca/airshows/index.htm

History and Heritage

Peacekeeping
http://www.achq.dnd.ca/peacekpg/index.htm

VJ-Day
http://www.achq.dnd.ca/vjday/vjday.htm

Avro Arrow
http://calum.csclub.uwaterloo.ca/u/rkschmid/Arrow/AvroArrow.html

Air Command Headquarters Museum
http://www.achq.dnd.ca/atrium/index.htm

Various Air Museums
http://www.achq.dnd.ca/museums.htm

Canadian Aerospace Training Project
http://www.dnd.ca/cfinfo/fdev/catp/welcome.html

About Astronaut and Air Force Major Chris Hadfield
http://www.achq.dnd.ca/roundel/dec95/hadfld.htm

Operations and Exercises

Operation Pivot
(Haiti)
http://bbs.cfcsc.dnd.ca/Oppivot/pivot.html

Operation Lance
(Rwanda)
http://bbs.cfcsc.dnd.ca/Op_Lance/lance.html

Peace and Security WWW Server
http://www.cfcsc.dnd.ca

Aerospace Engineering and Test Establishment
http://www.achq.dnd.ca/aete/index.htm

Canadian Forces School of Aerospace Studies
http://www.achq.dnd.ca/cfsas/cfsas.htm

Royal Canadian Air Cadets
http://www.isisnet.com/smacdouga/rcac/rcac.html

CANADIAN NAVY
http://www.dnd.ca/navy/index_e.htm

Maritime Command
http://www.marlant.halifax.dnd.ca/cdnnavy.html

About Maritime Command
http://www.marlant.halifax.dnd.ca/marcom.html

Vision
http://www.marlant.halifax.dnd.ca/vision.html

Mission
http://www.marlant.halifax.dnd.ca/part1vd.html

Navy Ships
http://www.marlant.halifax.dnd.ca/shipse.html

HALIFAX Class Frigates
http://www.marlant.halifax.dnd.ca/halifax.html

IROQUOIS Class Destroyers
http://www.marlant.halifax.dnd.ca/iroquois.html

ANNAPOLIS Class Destroyers
http://www.marlant.halifax.dnd.ca/annapoli.html

Improved Restigouche Class Destroyers
http://www.marlant.halifax.dnd.ca/restigou.html

OBERON Class Submarines
http://www.marlant.halifax.dnd.ca/oberons.html

KINGSTON Class Coastal Defence Vessels
http://www.marlant.halifax.dnd.ca/kingston.html

Operational Support Ships
http://www.marlant.halifax.dnd.ca/tankers.html

Minesweepers — Auxiliary
http://www.marlant.halifax.dnd.ca/msae.html

Warfare Centre
http://www.marlant.halifax.dnd.ca/cfmwce.html

MATELOT Online Newsletter
http://www.marlant.halifax.dnd.ca/matelote.html

Photographs
http://www.marlant.halifax.dnd.ca/photbank.html

Badges
http://www.marlant.halifax.dnd.ca/badges.html

HMCS *Sackville*
(Naval memorial)
http://fox.nstn.ca/~nstn1674

Naval Museum of Alberta
http://www.lexicom.ab.ca/~navalmuseum/navalmuseum.html

Allied Command Atlantic
http://www.saclant.nato.int/

Maritime Command Pacific
http://www.islandnet.com/%7Ebpaoesq/toc.htm

General Information
http://www.islandnet.com/%7Ebpaoesq/back.htm

CFB Esquimalt
http://www.islandnet.com/%7Ebpaoesq/homepage.htm

Arabian Gulf Multinational Interception Force
http://www.islandnet.com/%7Ebpaoesq/arabia.htm

Canadian Naval Presence in Asia-Pacific Region
http://www.islandnet.com/%7Ebpaoesq/asia.htm

Victoria Rescue Coordination Centre
http://www.islandnet.com/%7Ebpaoesq/rcc.htm

Ships' Movements
(Weekly)
http://www.islandnet.com/%7Ebpaoesq/shipmove.htm

West Coast Patrols
http://www.islandnet.com/%7Ebpaoesq/canpat.htm

Operation Sharp Guard in the Adriatic
http://www.islandnet.com/%7Ebpaoesq/sharp.htm

About Bay Class Patrol Boats
http://www.islandnet.com/%7Ebpaoesq/bayc.htm

About Ships and Aircraft
http://www.islandnet.com/%7Ebpaoesq/fact.htm

Relevant Links
http://www.islandnet.com/%7Ebpaoesq/links.htm

CANADIAN ARMY
http://www.lfc.dnd.ca/english/index.htm

Organization
http://www.lfc.dnd.ca/english/organis/index.htm

Operational Missions
http://www.lfc.dnd.ca/english/oper/index.htm

Public Affairs
http://www.lfc.dnd.ca/english/publ/index.htm

Military Equipment
http://www.lfc.dnd.ca/english/equip/index.htm

Site Map
http://www.lfc.dnd.ca/english/plan.htm

Photo Archives
http://www.lfc.dnd.ca/english/photos/index.htm

RESERVES AND CADETS
http://www.dnd.ca/rescad/index_e.htm

Special Restructuring Commission
http://www.dnd.ca/cfinfo/crc/scrr/scrr_e.html

CANADIAN FORCES COLLEGE
http://hermes.cfcsc.dnd.ca/

About the College
http://hermes.cfcsc.dnd.ca/info.html

Information Resource Centre
http://www.cfcsc.dnd.ca/welcome.html

OPERATION ALLIANCE
(Bosnia)
http://hermes.cfcsc.dnd.ca/Alliance/alliance.html

COMMUNICATIONS SECURITY ESTABLISHMENT
http://www.cse.dnd.ca/

Information Technology Security (INFOSEC) Mission
http://www.cse.dnd.ca/MandM/English/Mission.html

Mandate
http://www.cse.dnd.ca/MandM/English/Mandate.html

Services
http://www.cse.dnd.ca/Services/Services.html

Guide to Security Risk Management in Information Technology Systems (SRMITS)
http://www.cse.dnd.ca/Services/TRA/SRMITS/English/SRMITS.html

Learning Centre
http://www.cse.dnd.ca/English/ITS.html

Documentation
http://www.cse.dnd.ca/Services/Documentation/English/docenglish.html

Trusted Computer Product Evaluation
http://www.cse.dnd.ca/Services/Criteria/English/Criteria.html

Research and Development
http://www.cse.dnd.ca/Services/RandD/RandD.html

Public Key Infrastructure and Information Technology Security
http://www.cse.dnd.ca/PKI/gocpki_e.htm

CAR ITS Strategy
http://www.cse.dnd.ca/GOCITSTRATEGY/index.html

Relevant CSE Links
http://www.cse.dnd.ca/Others/Others.html

MILITARY-RELATED LINKS AROUND THE WORLD
http://www.dnd.ca/othlinks.htm

National Energy Board

http://canada.gc.ca/depts/agencies/nebind_e.html

The National Energy Board regulates oil, gas, and electricity in Canada.

This site is not yet fully developed at the time of publication of this book and offers limited information pertaining to the board's mandate and field of responsibility.

National Farm Products Marketing Council

http://aceis.agr.ca/./nfpce.html

The National Farm Products Marketing Council relates to agencies operating under the Farm Products Agencies Act.

This site is not yet fully developed at the time of publication of this book and offers limited information pertaining to the council's mandate and field of responsibility.

National Film Board

http://www.nfb.ca/

ABOUT THE NFB
http://www.nfb.ca/E/1/

ORGANIZATION
http://www.nfb.ca/E/2/

NFB COLLECTION
http://www.nfb.ca/E/4/2/

OSCAR WINNERS
http://www.nfb.ca/E/2/6/2/oscars.html

PRODUCTION
http://www.nfb.ca/E/3/

DISTRIBUTION
http://www.nfb.ca/E/4/

Locations
http://www.nfb.ca/E/4/partners.html

STOCKSHOT LIBRARY
http://www.nfb.ca/E/4/3/

Collection
http://www.nfb.ca/E/4/3/1/

Ordering
http://www.nfb.ca/E/4/3/6/index.html

National Gallery of Canada

http://national.gallery.ca/

ABOUT THE GALLERY
(Information about gallery hours, admission, parking, food services, tours, group rates, etc.)
http://national.gallery.ca/genlis.html

MEMBERSHIP
http://national.gallery.ca/rmember.html

HISTORY
http://national.gallery.ca/history.html

TABLE OF CONTENTS
http://national.gallery.ca/eindex.html

EXHIBITIONS
http://national.gallery.ca/exiblis.html

BOOKSTORE
http://national.gallery.ca/book.html

EVENTS AND PROGRAMS
http://national.gallery.ca/frmevent.html

LIBRARY AND ARCHIVE
http://national.gallery.ca/library.html

MUSEUM OF CONTEMPORARY PHOTOGRAPHY
http://national.gallery.ca/cmcp.html

National Library of Canada

http://www.nlc-bnc.ca/

WHAT'S NEW
http://www.nlc-bnc.ca/ewotsnew.htm

PRESS RELEASES
http://www.nlc-bnc.ca/pubs/press/epress.htm

TABLE OF CONTENTS
http://www.nlc-bnc.ca/ehome.htm

THE NATIONAL LIBRARIAN
http://www.nlc-bnc.ca/escotmes.htm

MANDATE
http://www.nlc-bnc.ca/emandate.htm

ANNUAL REPORT
http://www.nlc-bnc.ca/pubs/annrep95/94ann-e.htm

TOURING THE FACILITY
http://www.nlc-bnc.ca/vtour/evtour.htm

COLLECTIONS AND SERVICES
http://www.nlc-bnc.ca/services/nlindex.htm

RESOURCE SHARING
http://www.nlc-bnc.ca/resource/resha-e.htm

NLC ELECTRONIC PUBLICATIONS PILOT PROJECT
http://www.nlc-bnc.ca/eppp/e3pe.htm

PUBLISHING

http://www.nlc-bnc.ca/pubs/epub-pro.htm

PUBLICATIONS

http://www.nlc-bnc.ca/pubs/epubs.htm

PUBLIC PROGRAMS

Exhibitions and Displays

http://www.nlc-bnc.ca/events/exhibits.htm

Lectures and Readings

http://www.nlc-bnc.ca/events/readings/epodium.htm

Events

http://www.nlc-bnc.ca/pubs/pp-broch/febcal-e.htm

BECOME A FRIEND OF THE NATIONAL LIBRARY

http://www.nlc-bnc.ca/efriends.htm

BOUTIQUE

http://www.nlc-bnc.ca/eboutiqu.htm

THE NATIONAL LIBRARY NEWS

(Newsletter)

http://www.nlc-bnc.ca/publications/nl-news/enlnews.htm

AMICUS BIBLIOGRAPHIC RECORDS

http://www.nlc-bnc.ca/amicus/access/eaccamic.htm

National Museum of Science and Technology

http://www.nmstc.ca/

ABOUT THE MUSEUM
http://www.nmstc.ca/nmst/muse/egeninfo.htm

EDUCATIONAL PROGRAMS
http://www.nmstc.ca/nmst/educ/eeducgen.htm

EXHIBITS
http://www.nmstc.ca/nmst/exhibit/eexibntr.htm

RESEARCH RESOURCES
http://www.nmstc.ca/nmst/research/eresres.htm

NATIONAL AVIATION MUSEUM
http://www.nmstc.ca/nam/index.htm

AGRICULTURE MUSEUM
http://www.nmstc.ca/ag/index.htm

National Parole Board

http://canada.gc.ca/depts/agencies/npbind_e.html

The National Parole Board website offers general information pertaining to its mandate, mission, and program objective. Visitors will also find information relating to conditional release, clemency, and pardons.

National Research Council Canada

http://www.corpserv.nrc.ca/

WHAT'S NEW
http://www.corpserv.nrc.ca/corpserv/n_main_e.html

TABLE OF CONTENTS
http://www.corpserv.nrc.ca/corpserv/nrc.html

OPPORTUNITIES
http://www.corpserv.nrc.ca/corpserv/o_main_e.html

EMPLOYMENT OPPORTUNITIES
http://www.corpserv.nrc.ca/corpserv/o_empl_e.html

RESEARCH ASSOCIATESHIPS PROGRAM
http://www.corpserv.nrc.ca/corpserv/o_ra_e.html

WOMEN IN ENGINEERING AND SCIENCE (WES) PROGRAM
http://www.corpserv.nrc.ca/corpserv/g_wes_e.html

SUMMER EMPLOYMENT PROGRAM
http://www.corpserv.nrc.ca/corpserv/g_post_e.html

UPCOMING TRADE SHOWS
http://www.corpserv.nrc.ca/corpserv/t_main_e.html

INTERNATIONAL SCIENCE AND
TECHNOLOGY CONFERENCES
http://www.corpserv.nrc.ca/corpserv/o_intr_e.html

INDUSTRIAL RESEARCH ASSISTANCE PROGRAMS
http://www.irap.nrc.ca/irap/irap.html

GALLERY
http://www.corpserv.nrc.ca/corpserv/v_main_e.html

CANADIAN SCIENCE AND ENGINEERING HALL OF FAME
http://www.corpserv.nrc.ca/corpserv/hall/u_main_e.html

DIRECTORY OF NATIONAL RESEARCH COUNCIL STAFF
http://www.corpserv.nrc.ca/corpserv/k_pho_e.html

DIRECTORY OF S&T-RELATED SITES
http://www.corpserv.nrc.ca/corpserv/k_site_e.html

RESEARCH INFORMATION

Institutes, Technology Centres, Locations, News, Etc.
http://www.corpserv.nrc.ca/corpserv/m_list_e.html

ARCHIVES
http://www.corpserv.nrc.ca/corpserv/a_main_e.html

FOR STUDENTS
http://www.corpserv.nrc.ca/corpserv/g_main_e.html

SEND YOUR COMMENTS
Email: r&d@nrc.ca

National Transportation Agency of Canada

http://www.nta-ont.gc.ca/

MANDATE
http://www.nta-ont.gc.ca/eng/general/backeng.htm

AIR TRANSPORTATION
http://www.nta-ont.gc.ca/eng/air/aatb.htm

RAIL TRANSPORTATION
http://www.nta-ont.gc.ca/eng/rail/railb.htm

MARINE TRANSPORTATION
http://www.nta-ont.gc.ca/eng/marine/marineb.htm

MOTOR VEHICLE
http://www.nta-ont.gc.ca/eng/toc.htm#motor vehicle

DECISIONS
http://www.nta-ont.gc.ca/eng/dec96/numbers.htm

ORDERS
http://www.nta-ont.gc.ca/eng/orders96/intro.htm

HOW TO CONTACT THEM
http://www.nta-ont.gc.ca/eng/general/contacts.htm

Natural Resources Canada

http://www.NRCan.gc.ca/

THE HON. ANN MCLELLAN, MINISTER
http://www.NRCan.gc.ca/home/minister.htm

TABLE OF CONTENTS
http://www.NRCan.gc.ca/home/nrcanhpe.htm

ABOUT THE DEPARTMENT
http://www.emr.ca/hqlib/public.htm

DEPARTMENTAL OVERVIEW
http://www.NRCan.gc.ca/home/nrcan.htm

EMPLOYEE DIRECTORY
http://www.NRCan.gc.ca/home/phonee.htm

THE SOURCE
(Departmental newsletter)
http://www.NRCan.gc.ca/source/

GEOLOGICAL SURVEY OF CANADA
http://www.emr.ca/gsc/

GEOMATICS CANADA
http://www.geocan.NRCan.gc.ca/

POLAR CONTINENTAL SHELF PROJECT
http://www.emr.ca/gsc/pcsp/pcsp.html

CANADIAN EARTHQUAKE INFORMATION
http://www.seismo.emr.ca/

NATIONAL ATLAS INFORMATION
http://www-nais.ccm.NRCan.gc.ca/

DEFACTO — GEOGRAPHICAL INFORMATION
http://www-nais.ccm.emr.ca/defacto/

NATIONAL POLLUTANT RELEASE INVENTORY
http://www-nais.ccm.NRCan.gc.ca/npri/npri_e.html

AERONAUTICAL CHARTS SERVICE
http://www.geocan.NRCan.gc.ca/~aero/

CANADA CENTRE FOR REMOTE SENSING
http://www.ccrs.NRCan.gc.ca/

SERVICES TO THE PUBLIC
gopher://gopher.emr.ca:70/00/NRCan-Info-English/services

RELATED USENET NEWSGROUPS
nrcan.general
nrcan.networks

DIRECTORY OF EMPLOYEES
http://www.NRCan.gc.ca/home/phonee.htm

SEND YOUR COMMENTS
http://www.NRCan.gc.ca/home/comfor-e.htm
http://www.nserc.ca/index.htm

Natural Sciences and Engineering Research Council of Canada

ABOUT NSERC
http://www.nserc.ca/fact.htm

NEWS RELEASES
http://www.nserc.ca/news1.htm

CANADIAN RESEARCH SUCCESS STORIES
http://www.nserc.ca/great.htm

PROGRAMS
http://www.nserc.ca/programs.htm

GRANTS
http://www.nserc.ca/programs/grcoune.htm

INTERNATIONAL RELATIONS
http://www.nserc.ca/inter.htm

FORMS
http://www.nserc.ca/forms.htm

PUBLICATIONS
http://www.nserc.ca/publicat.htm

COMMITTEES
http://www.nserc.ca/comme.htm

STAFF DIRECTORY
http://www.nserc.ca/usrdatabase/nserc1.html

HOTLIST
http://www.nserc.ca/relate.htm

Northern Pipeline Canada

http://canada.gc.ca/depts/agencies/npaind_e.html

Northern Pipeline Canada is responsible for the Canadian portion of the Alaska Highway Gas Pipeline Project.

This site is not yet fully developed at the time of publication of this book and offers limited information pertaining to the agency's mandate and field of responsibility.

Northwest Territories Water Board

http://canada.gc.ca/depts/agencies/ntwind_e.html

The Northwest Territories Water Board focuses on the water resources of the Northwest Territories.

This site is not yet fully developed at the time of publication of this book and offers limited information pertaining to the board's mandate and field of responsibility.

Office of the Information Commissioner

http://infoweb.magi.com/~accessca/index.html

INTRODUCTION
http://infoweb.magi.com/~accessca/what_e.html

ROLE
http://infoweb.magi.com/~accessca/who_e.html

FREQUENTLY ASKED QUESTIONS
http://infoweb.magi.com/~accessca/brochure.html

ADDRESS
http://infoweb.magi.com/~accessca/address.html

Office of the Inspector General of the Canadian Security Intelligence Service

http://canada.gc.ca/depts/agencies/oigind_e.html

The Office of the Inspector General of the Canadian Security Intelligence Service monitors and reviews the operations of CSIS.

This site is not yet fully developed at the time of publication of this book and offers limited information pertaining to the office's mandate and field of responsibility.

Office of the Privacy Commissioner

http://infoweb.magi.com/~privcan/

BRUCE PHILLIPS, PRIVACY COMMISSIONER
http://infoweb.magi.com/~privcan/bruce.html

WHAT'S NEW
http://infoweb.magi.com/~privcan/new.html

OVERVIEW
http://infoweb.magi.com/~privcan/whatwedo.html

THE PRIVACY ACT
http://infoweb.magi.com/~privcan/act.html

PUBLICATIONS
http://infoweb.magi.com/~privcan/pubs.html

HOW TO REACH THEM
http://infoweb.magi.com/~privcan/reachus.html

PRIVACY-RELATED HOTLINKS
http://infoweb.magi.com/~privcan/other.html

PRIVACY AND THE CENSUS
http://infoweb.magi.com/~privcan/pubs/census.html

Office of the Superintendent of Financial Institutions Canada

http://canada.gc.ca/depts/agencies/sfiind_e.html

The Office of the Superintendent of Financial Institutions Canada supervises financial institutions in Canada.

This site is not yet fully developed at the time of publication of this book and offers limited information pertaining to the office's mandate and field of responsibility.

Pacific Pilotage Authority Canada

http://canada.gc.ca/depts/agencies/ppaind_e.html

Pacific Pilotage Authority Canada offers services within coastal waters of British Columbia and the Fraser River. A Crown corporation, it is one of four pilotage authorities in Canada.

This site is not yet fully developed at the time of publication of this book and offers limited information pertaining to the authority's mandate and field of responsibility.

Passport Office

http://www.ncf.carleton.ca/freeport/government/federal/passport/menu

WHAT'S NEW

http://www.ncf.carleton.ca/freenet/rootdir/menus/government/federal/passport/announce

ABOUT THE PASSPORT OFFICE

http://www.ncf.carleton.ca/freenet/rootdir/menus/government/federal/passport/about

HOW TO GET A PASSPORT

In Canada

http://www.ncf.carleton.ca/freenet/rootdir/menus/government/federal/passport/canada

In the USA

http://www.ncf.carleton.ca/freenet/rootdir/menus/government/federal/passport/USA

In Other Countries

http://www.ncf.carleton.ca/freenet/rootdir/menus/government/federal/passport/outside

ABOUT YOUR PASSPORT

http://www.ncf.carleton.ca/freenet/rootdir/menus/government/federal/passport/passport

PASSPORT OFFICES

National Capital Region

http://www.ncf.carleton.ca/freenet/rootdir/menus/government/federal/passport/ncr

Outside the National Capital Region

http://www.ncf.carleton.ca/freenet/rootdir/menus/government/federal/passport/locations

FEES

http://www.ncf.carleton.ca/freenet/rootdir/menus/government/federal/passport/fees

LOST OR STOLEN PASSPORTS

http://www.ncf.carleton.ca/freenet/rootdir/menus/government/federal/passport/loss

STATELESS PERSONS OR REFUGEES

http://www.ncf.carleton.ca/freenet/rootdir/menus/government/federal/passport/refugees

Patented Medicine Prices Review Board Canada

http://canada.gc.ca/depts/agencies/pmpind_e.html

Patented Medicine Prices Review Board Canada monitors price trends in the pharmaceutical industry.

This site is not yet fully developed at the time of publication of this book and offers limited information pertaining to the board's mandate and field of responsibility.

Pension Appeals Board

http://canada.gc.ca/depts/agencies/pabind_e.html

This site is not yet fully developed at the time of publication of this book and offers limited information pertaining to the board's mandate and field of responsibility.

Privy Council Office

http://canada.gc.ca/depts/agencies/pcoind_e.html

STATEMENT BY MINISTER OF INTERGOVERNMENTAL AFFAIRS
http://canada.gc.ca/depts/agencies/stat_e.html

Public Service Commission of Canada

http://www.psc-cfp.gc.ca/subpage.htm

ABOUT THE COMMISSION
http://www.psc-cfp.gc.ca/mission/whoweare.htm

OVERVIEW
http://www.psc-cfp.gc.ca/mission/comeng.htm

MISSION STATEMENT
http://www.psc-cfp.gc.ca/mission/pscmise.htm

FREQUENTLY ASKED QUESTIONS
http://www.psc-cfp.gc.ca/mission/sorry1.htm

EMPLOYMENT OPPORTUNITIES
http://www.psc-cfp.gc.ca/recruit/cfp1e.htm

International
http://www.psc-cfp.gc.ca/intpgm/epb1.htm

JOB OPPORTUNITIES ACROSS CANADA
http://www.psc-cfp.gc.ca/recruit/cfp5e.htm

By Geographical Area
http://www.psc-cfp.gc.ca/recruit/cfp6e.htm

Quebec
http://www.psc-cfp.gc.ca/recruit/cfp10e.htm

National Capital and Eastern Ontario
http://www.psc-cfp.gc.ca/recruit/cfp8e.htm

Specific Positions
http://www.psc-cfp.gc.ca/recruit/cfp7e.htm

Find employment information including job titles, tenure, location, requirements, salary, and application deadline.

HOW AND WHERE TO APPLY
http://www.psc-cfp.gc.ca/recruit/cfp9e.htm

This site provides relevant details and links to important PSC telephone numbers in your area.

A WORD ABOUT PUBLIC SERVICE RECRUITMENT
http://www.psc-cfp.gc.ca/recruit/cfp2e.htm

HOW TO APPLY
Federal Summer Student Employment Program
http://www.psc-cfp.gc.ca/recruit/fssep1e.htm

Post-Secondary Recruitment
http://www.psc-cfp.gc.ca/recruit/psrhome.htm

Management Trainee Program
http://www.psc-cfp.gc.ca/recruit/psceng.htm

Development Officer Recruitment Program for CIDA
http://www.psc-cfp.gc.ca/recruit/cidae.htm

Aboriginal Master's Program
http://www.psc-cfp.gc.ca/recruit/ianeng.htm

Recruitment-Related Sites
http://www.psc-cfp.gc.ca/recruit/psrhome.htm

Recruitment Newsletter
http://www.psc-cfp.gc.ca/recruit/cfp12e.htm

DIVERSITY MANAGEMENT
http://www.psc-cfp.gc.ca/dmd/dmd_0.htm

TRAINING PRODUCTS AND SERVICES
http://www.edu.psc-cfp.gc.ca/

ANNUAL REPORT
http://www.psc-cfp.gc.ca/annrept/ann9495e.htm

SEND YOUR COMMENTS
Email: Info-Com@MS.PSC-CFP.X400.GC.CA

Public Service Staff Relations Board

http://canada.gc.ca/depts/agencies/srbind_e.html

The Public Service Staff Relations Board relates to the rights and responsibilities of the employers and employees in the federal public service.

This site is not yet fully developed at the time of publication of this book and offers limited information pertaining to the board's mandate and field of responsibility.

Public Works and Government Services Canada

http://w3.pwgsc.gc.ca/

TABLE OF CONTENTS
http://w3.pwgsc.gc.ca/text/home-e.html

WHAT'S NEW
http://w3.pwgsc.gc.ca/text/whats-e.html

PRESS RELEASES
http://www.newswire.ca/cgi-bin/organization.cgi?ref=pubw

OVERVIEW
http://w3.pwgsc.gc.ca/text/oursite.html

THE MINISTER, HON. DIANE MARLEAU
http://w3.pwgsc.gc.ca/text/marleaue.html

BRANCHES AND AGENCIES
http://w3.pwgsc.gc.ca/text/englsh-e.html

Communications Branch
http://w3.pwgsc.gc.ca/comm/text/chm-e.html

Government Telecommunications and Informatics Services
http://w3.pwgsc.gc.ca/gtis/text/org-e.html

Real Property Services Branch
http://w3.pwgsc.gc.ca/text/realp-e.html

Supply Operations Service Branch
http://w3.pwgsc.gc.ca/text/sos-e.html

R&D BULLETIN
http://w3.pwgsc.gc.ca/rdbullet/text/martoc.html

INTERNATIONAL NETWORK ON ACCESSIBILITY
http://w3.pwgsc.gc.ca/text/accesse.html

PACIFIC ACQUISITIONS ONLINE SERVICE
http://w3.pwgsc.gc.ca/nmsovan/index.html

ARCHITECTURAL AND ENGINEERING SERVICES
http://w3.pwgsc.gc.ca/text/aes-e.html

DEPOSITORY SERVICE PROGRAM
http://www.ccg-gcc.ca/dsp-psd/index-e.html

CANADA COMMUNICATION GROUP
http://www.ccg-gcc.ca/

Publishing
http://www.ccg-gcc.ca/publishing/index-e.html

DOING BUSINESS WITH PWGSC
http://w3.pwgsc.gc.ca/comm/text/dbintro.html

OPEN BIDDING SERVICE
http://www.obs.ism.ca/

RECEIVER GENERAL OF CANADA
http://w3.pwgsc.gc.ca/text/recgen-e.html

TELEPHONE DIRECTORY
http://w3.pwgsc.gc.ca/text/phone-e.html

HOTEL AND CAR RENTAL DIRECTORY FOR GOVERNMENT EMPLOYEES
http://w3.pwgsc.gc.ca/hotelcar/

PROPERTY FOR SALE
http://w3.pwgsc.gc.ca/govland/

SUPPLIER PROMOTION PROGRAM
http://w3.pwgsc.gc.ca/ccsp

TRANSLATION BUREAU
http://w3.pwgsc.gc.ca/termium/

SEND YOUR COMMENTS
http://w3.pwgsc.gc.ca/text/cmts-e.html

Revenue Canada

http://www.revcan.ca/

WHAT'S NEW
http://www.revcan.ca/menu/EmenuBAA.html

THE HON. JANE STEWART, MINISTER
http://www.revcan.ca/minister.html

PRESS RELEASES AND SPEECHES
http://www.revcan.ca/menu/EmenuMZZ.html

ABOUT THE DEPARTMENT
http://www.revcan.ca/menu/EmenuDAA.html

INDEX TO SERVICES
http://www.revcan.ca/~paulb/service/content1.htm

Taxes
http://www.revcan.ca/~paulb/service/content2.htm#CHAP2TAX

Canada Customs
http://www.revcan.ca/~paulb/service/content2.htm#CHAP3CUS

Small Business Services
http://www.revcan.ca/~paulb/service/content2.htm#CHAP4SRV

SPECIAL SERVICES
http://www.revcan.ca/menu/EmenuDBA.html

Volunteer Information Sheet
http://www.revcan.ca/E/pbg/fm/xt242p/README.html

Government Services
http://www.revcan.ca/E/pub/gd/et4069a/t4069e.html

Goods and Services Tax (GST)
http://www.revcan.ca/E/pub/gd/et4071a/t4071e.html

Rulings Directorate Service
http://www.revcan.ca/E/pub/gd/et4122a/et4122.html

Small Business Information Seminar
http://www.revcan.ca/E/pub/gd/et4075a/t4075e.html

International Publications
http://www.revcan.ca/E/pub/gd/et41252a/README.html

Teaching Taxes Seminar — Workbook
http://www.revcan.ca/E/pub/gd/etis17a/tis17e94.html

Teaching Taxes Program — Teacher's Manual
http://www.revcan.ca/E/pub/gd/etis18a/README.html

FREQUENTLY ASKED QUESTIONS
http://www.revcan.ca/menu/EmenuCAA.html

PUBLICATIONS
http://www.revcan.ca/menu/EmenuGZA.html

Students and Income Tax
http://www.revcan.ca/~paulb/html/student.htm

I Declare
http://www.revcan.ca/~paulb/html/declare.htm

Tables on Diskette
(Mac, DOS, Windows)
http://www.revcan.ca/tod/tablese.html

INFORMATION FOR BUSINESS
http://www.revcan.ca/menu/EmenuHZZ.html

INFORMATION FOR INDIVIDUALS
http://www.revcan.ca/menu/EmenuGZZ.html

INFORMATION FOR NON-RESIDENTS
http://www.revcan.ca/menu/EmenuIZZ.html

INFORMATION FOR CHARITIES
http://www.revcan.ca/menu/EmenuJAA.html

TECHNICAL INFORMATION
http://www.revcan.ca/menu/EmenuKZZ.html

FORMS
http://www.revcan.ca/menu/EmenuLZZ.html

HOTLINKS
http://www.revcan.ca/menu/EmenuMJZ.html

Royal Canadian Mint

http://www.rcmint.ca/

THE NEW $2 COIN
http://www.rcmint.ca/rcm/eternal/main.html

COLLECTOR COINS
http://www.rcmint.ca/rcm/catalog/open.html

PRESS RELEASES
http://www.rcmint.ca/rcm/newsrel.html

ABOUT THE ROYAL CANADIAN MINT
http://www.rcmint.ca/rcm/about/about.html

HISTORY
http://www.rcmint.ca/rcm/about/history.html

THE MINT TODAY
http://www.rcmint.ca/rcm/about/today.html

THE MASTER OF THE MINT
http://www.rcmint.ca/rcm/about/whoswho.html

VISITING THE MINT IN OTTAWA
http://www.rcmint.ca/rcm/about/ottawa.html

VISITING THE MINT IN WINNIPEG
http://www.rcmint.ca/rcm/about/winnipeg.html

BULLION INVESTMENT COINS
http://www.rcmint.ca/rcm/eternal/gold/index.html

Bullion
http://www.rcmint.ca/rcm/eternal/gold/bullion.html

Platinum
http://www.rcmint.ca/rcm/eternal/gold/platinum.html

Gold
http://www.rcmint.ca/rcm/eternal/gold/gold.html

Silver
http://www.rcmint.ca/rcm/eternal/gold/silver.html

REFINERY SERVICES
http://www.rcmint.ca/rcm/eternal/gold/refinery.html

GLOSSARY
http://www.rcmint.ca/rcm/eternal/gold/glossary.html

Royal Canadian Mounted Police

http://www.rcmp-grc.gc.ca/

PRESS RELEASES
http://www.rcmp-grc.gc.ca/html/press.htm

TABLE OF CONTENTS
http://www.rcmp-grc.gc.ca/html/tableof.htm

RCMP PUBLIC COMPLAINTS COMMISSION
http://canada.gc.ca/depts/agencies/pccind_e.html

The RCMP Public Complaints Commission is an independent body.

RCMP EXTERNAL REVIEW COMMITTEE
http://canada.gc.ca/depts/agencies/ercind_e.html

The RCMP External Review Committee is an independent body.

ABORIGINAL POLICING
http://www.rcmp-grc.gc.ca/html/aborig.htm

CADET TRAINING
http://www.rcmp-grc.gc.ca/html/cadets.htm

CANADIAN POLICE COLLEGE
http://www.rcmp-grc.gc.ca/html/cpc.htm

CANADIAN POLICE INFORMATION CENTRE
http://www.rcmp-grc.gc.ca/html/cpic.htm

CANADIAN POLICE RESEARCH CENTRE
http://www.rcmp-grc.gc.ca/html/resear.htm

COASTAL WATCH/AIRPORT WATCH
http://www.rcmp-grc.gc.ca/html/cwatch-e.htm

COMMERCIAL CRIME
http://www.rcmp-grc.gc.ca/html/commerc.htm

COMMISSIONER'S DIRECTIONAL STATEMENT
http://www.rcmp-grc.gc.ca/html/dir-stat.htm

COMMUNITY POLICING
http://www.rcmp-grc.gc.ca/html/com-pol.htm

COMMUNITY POLICING UNDER CONTRACT
http://www.rcmp-grc.gc.ca/html/contract.htm

COMMUNITY PROJECTS
http://www.rcmp-grc.gc.ca/html/mpfproj.htm

COMPUTER AND TELECOMMUNICATIONS CRIME
http://www.rcmp-grc.gc.ca/html/cpu-cri.htm

COUNTERFEITING
http://www.rcmp-grc.gc.ca/html/counter.htm

CRIMINAL INTELLIGENCE PROGRAM
http://www.rcmp-grc.gc.ca/html/cr-intel.htm

CUSTOMS AND EXCISE PROGRAM
http://www.rcmp-grc.gc.ca/html/customs.htm

DETACHMENTS — FRONTLINE POLICING
http://www.rcmp-grc.gc.ca/html/detachm.htm

DIVISION STAFF RELATIONS REPRESENTATIVE
http://www.rcmp-grc.gc.ca/html/dsrr.htm

DNA CONSULTATION PAPER
http://www.rcmp-grc.gc.ca/html/dna-enew.htm

DRUG ENFORCEMENT
http://www.rcmp-grc.gc.ca/html/drugs.htm

FORENSIC LABORATORIES
http://www.rcmp-grc.gc.ca/html/labs.htm

HISTORY
http://www.rcmp-grc.gc.ca/html/history.htm

INFORMATION AND IDENTIFICATION SERVICES DIRECTORATE
http://www.rcmp-grc.gc.ca/html/ident.htm

IMMIGRATION, PASSPORT, AND CITIZENSHIP PROGRAM
http://www.rcmp-grc.gc.ca/html/imm.htm

INFORMATICS
http://www.rcmp-grc.gc.ca/html/inf-dir.htm

INTERNATIONAL LIAISON AND PROTECTIVE OPERATIONS
http://www.rcmp-grc.gc.ca/html/pr-ops.htm

INTERPOL
http://www.rcmp-grc.gc.ca/html/interpol.htm

Fugitives
http://www.rcmp-grc.gc.ca/html/fugits.htm

Stolen Cultural Property
http://www.rcmp-grc.gc.ca/html/arttheft.htm

List of Stolen Art
http://www.rcmp-grc.gc.ca/html/works.htm

LAND TRANSPORT, MARINE, AND AIR SERVICES
http://www.rcmp-grc.gc.ca/html/land-a-m.htm

MAGAZINES
RCMP Gazette
http://www.rcmp-grc.gc.ca/html/gazette.htm

Pony Express
http://www.rcmp-grc.gc.ca/html/pony.htm

The Quarterly
http://www.rcmp-grc.gc.ca/html/quarterl.htm

MISSION STATEMENT ON COMMUNITY POLICING
http://www.rcmp-grc.gc.ca/html/mission.htm

MOUNTED POLICE FOUNDATION
http://www.rcmp-grc.gc.ca/html/mpf-fct.htm

MUSICAL RIDE
http://www.rcmp-grc.gc.ca/html/ride.htm

ORGANIZATION
http://www.rcmp-grc.gc.ca/html/organiz.htm

Map
http://www.rcmp-grc.gc.ca/html/divmap.htm

OTHER FEDERAL PROGRAMS
http://www.rcmp-grc.gc.ca/html/othfed.htm

POLICE DOG SERVICES
http://www.rcmp-grc.gc.ca/html/dogs.htm

PROCEEDS OF CRIME
http://www.rcmp-grc.gc.ca/html/proceed.htm

PUBLICATIONS
http://www.rcmp-grc.gc.ca/html/pubctns.htm

Stopping Child Abuse — Protecting Our Future
http://www.rcmp-grc.gc.ca/html/abuse.htm

PATCH — Positive Action Teens Choosing Health
http://www.rcmp-grc.gc.ca/html/patch.htm

RECRUITING
http://www.rcmp-grc.gc.ca/html/recruit.htm

Contacts
http://www.rcmp-grc.gc.ca/html/recr-phs.htm

TECHNICAL SECURITY
http://www.rcmp-grc.gc.ca/html/tech.htm

TRAFFIC LAW ENFORCEMENT
http://www.rcmp-grc.gc.ca/html/traffic.htm

WAR CRIMES AND SPECIAL COMMENTS
http://www.rcmp-grc.gc.ca/html/warcrime.htm

SEND YOUR COMMENTS
http://www.rcmp-grc.gc.ca/html/mail.htm

St. Lawrence Seaway Authority

http://canada.gc.ca/depts/agencies/slsind_e.html

The St. Lawrence Seaway Authority operates the waterway between the Port of Montreal and Lake Erie.

This site is not yet fully developed at the time of publication of this book and offers limited information pertaining to the Seaway Authority's mandate and field of responsibility.

Security Intelligence Review Committee

http://canada.gc.ca/depts/agencies/sirind_e.html

The Security Intelligence Review Committee is an independent review body in relation to the Canadian Security Intelligence Service.

This site is not yet fully developed at the time of publication of this book and offers limited information pertaining to the committee's mandate and field of responsibility.

Social Sciences and Humanities Research Council of Canada

http://canada.gc.ca/depts/agencies/shrind_e.html

The Social Sciences and Humanities Research Council is a grant-giving body.

This site is not yet fully developed at the time of publication of this book and offers limited information pertaining to the council's mandate and field of responsibility.

Solicitor General of Canada

http://www.sgc.gc.ca/

THE SOLICITOR GENERAL
http://www.sgc.gc.ca/eministr.htp

ABOUT THE DEPARTMENT
http://www.sgc.gc.ca/department/eabout.htp

NEWS AND INFORMATION
http://www.sgc.gc.ca/news/enews.htp

REPORTS
http://www.sgc.gc.ca/ecopywri.htp

WHAT'S NEW
http://www.sgc.gc.ca/enew.htp

POLICING AND LAW ENFORCEMENT
http://www.sgc.gc.ca/depth/policing/epolice.htm

NATIONAL SECURITY
http://www.sgc.gc.ca/depth/national/enation.htp

CORRECTIONS
http://www.sgc.gc.ca/depth/corrections/ecorrect.htp

Standards Council of Canada

http://www.scc.ca/

WHAT'S NEW
http://www.scc.ca/whatsnew/index.html

PRESS RELEASES
http://www.scc.ca/pressrel/index.html

TABLE OF CONTENTS
http://www.scc.ca/indexe.html

ABOUT THE STANDARDS COUNCIL
http://www.scc.ca/about/index.html

PROGRAMS AND SERVICES
http://www.scc.ca/programs/index.html

INTERNATIONAL STANDARDIZATION
http://www.scc.ca/internat/index.html

CONSENSUS — CANADA'S NEWSMAGAZINE OF STANDARDIZATION
http://www.scc.ca/consensu/index.html

EMPLOYMENT OPPORTUNITIES
http://www.scc.ca/publicat/ad001.html

EVENTS
http://www.scc.ca/calendar/index.html

HOW TO REACH THEM
http://www.scc.ca/contact/index.html

Statistics Canada

http://www.statcan.ca/

TABLE OF CONTENTS
http://www.statcan.ca/start.html

WHAT'S NEW
http://www.statcan.ca/Documents/English/new.htm

THE DAILY
http://www.statcan.ca/Daily/English/today/daily.htm

ABOUT STATISTICS CANADA
http://www.statcan.ca/Documents/English/About/about.html

MAP AND LOCATIONS
http://www.statcan.ca/Reference/English/refcentre.html

STATISTICS ABOUT CANADA
http://www.statcan.ca/Documents/English/Faq/Glance/glance.htm

VIRTUAL LIBRARY
http://www.statcan.ca/Documents/English/Vlib/index.htm

Research Papers
http://www.statcan.ca/Documents/English/Vlib/Research/index.htm

Information by Subject
http://www.statcan.ca/Documents/English/Theme/index.htm

Catalogue
gopher://gopher.statcan.ca:70/11/.English/Products/Catalogs

Search Engine
http://www.statcan.ca/Reference/English/Search/search.html

INTERNET SERVICES
http://www.statcan.ca/Documents/English/Services/service.htm

About the Internet Service
http://www.statcan.ca/Documents/English/Services/aserv.htm

Gopher Service
gopher://gopher.statcan.ca:70/11/.English

ftp Service
ftp://ftp.statcan.ca/pub

List Server
http://www.statcan.ca/Reference/English/listserv.html

ELECTRONIC MARKETPLACE
http://www.statcan.ca/Documents/English/Commerce/index.htm

Databases
http://www.statcan.ca/Documents/English/Commerce/dbs.htm

Products and Services
http://www.statcan.ca/Documents/English/Commerce/pas.htm

Publications
http://www.statcan.ca/Documents/English/Commerce/pub.htm

STATISTICS HOTLINKS
http://www.statcan.ca/Reference/otherservers.html

TO ORDER INFORMATION
http://www.statcan.ca/cgi-bin/wwworder.pl

SEND YOUR COMMENTS
http://www.statcan.ca/cgi-bin/statcomment.pl

Status of Women Canada

http://canada.gc.ca/depts/agencies/swcind_e.html

Status of Women Canada promotes women's equality throughout Canadian life.

This site is not yet fully developed at the time of publication of this book and offers limited information pertaining to Status of Women Canada's mandate and field of responsibility.

Transport Canada

http://www.tc.gc.ca/

THE HON. DAVID ANDERSON, MINISTER
http://www.tc.gc.ca/cgi-bin/makehtm.exe?minister/anderson.txt
Email: mintc@tc.gc.ca

SPEECHES
http://www.tc.gc.ca/cgi-bin/makehtm.exe?tcgene~1/speeches.txt

NICK MULDER, DEPUTY MINISTER
http://www.tc.gc.ca/cgi-bin/makehtm.exe?deputyminister/nmulder.txt

PRESS RELEASES
http://www.tc.gc.ca/cgi-bin/makehtm.exe?tcgene~1/pressrel.txt

TABLE OF CONTENTS
http://www.tc.gc.ca/cgi-bin/makehtm.exe?tcgeneral/contents.txt

ABOUT THE DEPARTMENT
http://www.tc.gc.ca/cgi-bin/makehtm.exe?tcgene~1/overview.txt

ACTS AND REGULATIONS
http://www.tc.gc.ca/cgi-bin/makehtm.exe?Actsregs/welar.txt

CD-ROM and Diskette Versions
http://www.tc.gc.ca/actsregs/ele.htm

RESEARCH AND DEVELOPMENT
http://www.tc.gc.ca/cgi-bin/makehtm.exe?tcgeneral/r&d.txt

ROAD SAFETY INFORMATION
http://www.tc.gc.ca/cgi-bin/makehtm.exe?roadsaf/english/e-info.txt

AVIATION SAFETY INFORMATION
http://www.tc.gc.ca/cgi-bin/makehtm.exe?aviati~1/avsafety.txt

Aviation Safety Guide
http://www.tc.gc.ca/cgi-bin/makehtm.exe?aviati~1/english/bro.txt

SHIP SAFETY INFORMATION
http://www.tc.gc.ca/cgi-bin/makehtm.exe?shipsa~1/shiptoc.txt

CHEMICAL ACCIDENTS (CANUTEC)
http://www.tc.gc.ca/canutec/english/brochu-e.htm

TRANSPORTING DANGEROUS GOODS
http://www.tc.gc.ca/cgi-bin/makehtm.exe?tcgene~1/tdg_eng.txt

TELEPHONE DIRECTORY
http://www.tc.gc.ca/cgi-bin/makehtm.exe?tcphone/phone.txt

SEND YOUR COMMENTS
http://www.tc.gc.ca/cgi-bin/makehtm.exe?feedback/feedback.txt

Transportation Safety Board of Canada

http://www.bst-tsb.gc.ca/english.html

WHAT'S NEW
http://www.bst-tsb.gc.ca/whatsnew.html

MANDATE
http://www.bst-tsb.gc.ca/mandate.html

OFFICES
http://www.bst-tsb.gc.ca/offices.html

MARINE
http://www.bst-tsb.gc.ca/marinelist.html

PIPELINE
http://www.bst-tsb.gc.ca/pipelist.html

RAIL
http://www.bst-tsb.gc.ca/raillist.html

AIR
http://www.bst-tsb.gc.ca/airlist.html

SAFETY REPORTING PROGRAM
http://www.bst-tsb.gc.ca/securitase.html

PRESS RELEASES
http://www.bst-tsb.gc.ca/commun.html

GUEST BOOK
http://www.bst-tsb.gc.ca/guest.html

Treasury Board of Canada, Secretariat

http://www.tbs-sct.gc.ca/

WHAT'S NEW
http://www.tbs-sct.gc.ca/tb/whatnewe.html

PRESS RELEASES
http://www.tbs-sct.gc.ca/tb/newse/newse.html

SPEECHES
http://www.tbs-sct.gc.ca/tb/speeche/speeches.html

ABOUT THE TREASURY BOARD
http://www.tbs-sct.gc.ca/tb/tbinfoe.html

TABLE OF CONTENTS
http://www.tbs-sct.gc.ca/tb/home-eng.html

ESTIMATES OF THE GOVERNMENT OF CANADA
http://www.tbs-sct.gc.ca/tb/estimate/estime.html

PROGRAM PRIORITIES AND EXPENDITURES
http://www.tbs-sct.gc.ca/tb/pubs/out/oute.html

REPORTS TO PARLIAMENT
http://www.tbs-sct.gc.ca/tb/reps.html

PUBLICATIONS
http://www.tbs-sct.gc.ca/tb/pubs.html

BUREAU OF REAL PROPERTY AND MATERIAL
http://www.tbs-sct.gc.ca/tb/rp/brpm/brpm02e.html

INNOVATION AND QUALITY EXCHANGE
http://www.tbs-sct.gc.ca/tb/iqe/mnpgen.html

REGULATORY AFFAIRS
http://www.arraydev.com/tbs-rad/index.html

HOTLINKS
http://www.tbs-sct.gc.ca/tb/linkse.html

Veterans Affairs Canada

http://www.vac-acc.gc.ca/

THE HON. LAWRENCE MACAULAY, SECRETARY OF STATE
http://www.vac-acc.gc.ca/messages/secret~1.htm

DAVID NICHOLSON, DEPUTY MINISTER
http://www.vac-acc.gc.ca/messages/depmin.htm

MISSION AND MANDATE
http://www.vac-acc.gc.ca/mandate/mandate.htm

PROGRAMS
http://www.vac-acc.gc.ca/programs/progra-e.htm

CARILLON
(Monthly newsletter)
http://www.vac-acc.gc.ca/carillon/carillon.htm

COMMEMORATION
http://www.vac-acc.gc.ca/commem/commem-e.htm

BOOKS OF REMEMBRANCE
http://schoolnet2.carleton.ca/books/remember.htm

WAR MEMORIALS
http://www.vac-acc.gc.ca/commem/battfld/battles.htm

COMMEMORATION BOOKLETS
http://www.vac-acc.gc.ca/commem/booklet/booklst.htm

HISTORICAL ANECDOTES
http://www.vac-acc.gc.ca/commem/history/hist-eng.htm

Western Economic Diversification Canada

http://www.myriadgate.net/wd/

ABOUT WESTERN ECONOMIC DIVERSIFICATION
http://www.myriadgate.net/wd/english/services/wd.html

WHAT'S NEW
http://www.myriadgate.net/wd/english/press/index.html

AEROSPACE
http://www.myriadgate.net/wd/english/services/atci.html

AGRICULTURE
http://www.myriadgate.net/wd/english/services/avaf.html

BIO TECH
http://www.myriadgate.net/wd/english/services/babif.html

CAPITAL
http://www.myriadgate.net/wd/english/faq/finance.html

KNOWLEDGE-BASED INDUSTRY
http://www.myriadgate.net/wd/english/services/kbi.html

TOURISM
http://www.myriadgate.net/wd/english/services/tawnc.html

SITE MAP
http://www.myriadgate.net/cgi-bin/wd-nav/e

OFFICIAL LANGUAGE ACT
http://www.myriadgate.net/wd/english/press/ola/table.htm

Yukon Territory Water Board

http://canada.gc.ca/depts/agencies/ytwind_e.html

The Yukon Territory Water Board oversees the Yukon's surface and sub-surface water resources.

This site is not yet fully developed at the time of publication of this book and offers limited information pertaining to the board's mandate and field of responsibility.

The Provinces and Territories

Government Online in Canada

Introduction

You will find two lists here. The first one is a brief alphabetical listing of all provincial and territorial government sites. Pick a province, type in the appropriate URL, and you are there. It's that easy. The first web address is provided by the Government of Canada and offers general information about that particular province or territory. The next address is that particular province or territory's official homepage. Once there, simply follow the various online menus and instructions to make your way around.

The second list is much more comprehensive. It contains the most significant sites at each provincial or territorial website. Scan the list and type in the URL that most interests you. Once you have accessed it, you can follow the online site directives to move about that province's website.

You should enter the first two sites onto your browser's bookmarks. These sites are central staging points from which you can jump to each and every province and territory in Canada.

THE PROVINCES AND TERRITORIES
(Central federal government site)
http://canada.gc.ca/canadiana/proind_e.html

PROVINCIAL AND TERRITORIAL GOVERNMENTS
http://canada.gc.ca/othergov/prov_e.html

The Provinces and Territories in Brief

ALBERTA
http://canada.gc.ca/canadiana/faitc/proal_e.html
http://www.gov.ab.ca

BRITISH COLUMBIA
http://canada.gc.ca/canadiana/faitc/probc_e.html
http://www.gov.bc.ca

MANITOBA
http://canada.gc.ca/canadiana/faitc/proma_e.html
http://www.gov.mb.ca

NEW BRUNSWICK
http://canada.gc.ca/canadiana/faitc/pronb_e.html
http://www.gov.nb.ca/

NEWFOUNDLAND AND LABRADOR
http://canada.gc.ca/canadiana/faitc/pronf_e.html
http://www.gov.nf.ca/

NORTHWEST TERRITORIES
http://canada.gc.ca/canadiana/faitc/pronw_e.html
http://www.ssimicro.com/~xpsognwt/

NOVA SCOTIA
http://canada.gc.ca/canadiana/faitc/prons_e.html
http://www.gov.ns.ca/

ONTARIO
http://canada.gc.ca/canadiana/faitc/proon_e.html
http://www.gov.on.ca/

PRINCE EDWARD ISLAND
http://canada.gc.ca/canadiana/faitc/prope_e.html
http://www.gov.pe.ca/

QUEBEC
http://canada.gc.ca/canadiana/faitc/proqu_e.html
http://www.gouv.qc.ca/

SASKATCHEWAN
http://canada.gc.ca/canadiana/faitc/prosa_e.html
http://www.gov.sk.ca/

YUKON
http://canada.gc.ca/canadiana/faitc/proyu_e.html
No territorial homepage listed.

Alberta

http://www.gov.ab.ca/

PREMIER RALPH KLEIN
http://www.gov.ab.ca/gov/prem/premier.html

WHAT'S NEW
http://www.gov.ab.ca/whatsnew/index.html

PRESS RELEASES
http://www.gov.ab.ca/~pab/index.html

THE ALBERTA ADVANTAGE
http://www.gov.ab.ca/abadv.html

LEGISLATIVE ASSEMBLY
http://www.gov.ab.ca/gov/leg/index.html

MLA LISTING
http://www.gov.ab.ca/gov/leg/mla/indextbl.html

SPEECH FROM THE THRONE
http://www.gov.ab.ca/gov/speech/96throne.html

GOVERNMENT
http://www.gov.ab.ca/govt.html

GOVERNMENT DEPARTMENTS
http://www.gov.ab.ca/dept/dept.html

BOARDS, AGENCIES, COMMISSIONS, AND AUTHORITIES
http://www.gov.ab.ca/gov/agency/agency.html

BUDGET
http://www.treas.gov.ab.ca/comm/budget96/index.html

PEOPLE
http://www.gov.ab.ca/people.html

PROSPERITY
http://www.gov.ab.ca/prosp.html

PRESERVATION
http://www.gov.ab.ca/preserv.html

SEARCH ENGINE
http://www.gov.ab.ca/search.html

HOTLINKS
http://www.gov.ab.ca/misc/index.html

SEND YOUR COMMENTS
Email: AltaTalk@censsw.gov.ab.ca

British Columbia

http://www.gov.bc.ca/

WHAT'S NEW
http://www.gov.bc.ca/vtwm.html

PRESS RELEASES
http://www.gov.bc.ca/4dclient.acgi$nrindex

LEGISLATURE AND CONSTITUENCY INFORMATION
http://www.gov.bc.ca/os/os.html

LEGISLATIVE ASSEMBLY
http://www.legis.gov.bc.ca/

MEMBERS
http://www.legis.gov.bc.ca/mla_list.htm

HANSARD
http://www.legis.gov.bc.ca/hansard

SPEECH FROM THE THRONE
http://www.legis.gov.bc.ca/96throne.htm

MINISTRIES
http://www.gov.bc.ca/orgs/orgs.html

SOCIAL PROGRAMS
http://www.gov.bc.ca/sp/sp.html

BUSINESS
http://www.gov.bc.ca/business/business.html

BUDGET
http://www.fin.gov.bc.ca/budget96/budget96.htm

ENVIRONMENT
http://www.gov.bc.ca/envland/envland.html

TOURISM
http://www.gov.bc.ca/tourism/tourism.html

SEARCH ENGINE
http://www.gov.bc.ca/search/search.html

SEND YOUR COMMENTS
http://www.gov.bc.ca/feedback.html

Manitoba

http://www.gov.mb.ca/

PREMIER GARY FILMON
http://www.gov.mb.ca/text/quotepg1.html

WHAT'S NEW
http://www.gov.mb.ca/text/latest.html

PRESS RELEASES
http://www.gov.mb.ca/cgi-bin/List-News-Top

LEGISLATIVE ASSEMBLY
http://www.gov.mb.ca/leg-asmb/index.html

MEMBERS
http://www.gov.mb.ca/leg-asmb/hansard/6th-35th/memlist.html

HANSARD
http://www.gov.mb.ca/leg-asmb/hansard/index.html

VIRTUAL TOUR OF THE LEGISLATIVE BUILDING
http://www.gov.mb.ca/images/tour/index.html

SPEECH FROM THE THRONE
http://www.gov.mb.ca/leg-asmb/spek.html

DEPARTMENTS AND AGENCIES
http://www.gov.mb.ca/mb_index.html

FREEDOM OF INFORMATION ACCESS GUIDE
http://www.gov.mb.ca/accessguide.html

BUDGET
http://www.gov.mb.ca/finance/budget96.htm

MANITOBA INFORMATION HIGHWAY ADVISORY COUNCIL
http://www.gov.mb.ca/mihac/digital10.html

JOB POSTINGS
http://www.gov.mb.ca/cgi-bin/List-Jobs

TOURISM
http://www.gov.mb.ca/itt/travel/explore/index.html

KEY GOVERNMENT EMAIL ADDRESSES
http://www.gov.mb.ca/minister/index.html

GUEST BOOK
http://www.gov.mb.ca/guest_bk.html

New Brunswick

http://www.gov.nb.ca/

WHAT'S NEW
http://www.gov.nb.ca/whatsnew/index.htm

PRESS RELEASES, PHOTO FILE, CONFERENCES, FOREST FIRE UPDATES, AND MORE
http://www.gov.nb.ca/cnb/homenr.htm

PREMIER FRANK MCKENNA
http://www.gov.nb.ca/bios/mck-e.htm

PREMIER'S GREETING
http://www.gov.nb.ca/po/message.htm

Audio Message
http://www.gov.nb.ca/po/prem.wav

Video Message
http://www.gov.nb.ca/po/mckenna.mov

Premier's Virtual Office
http://www.gov.nb.ca/po/index.htm

Press Releases
http://www.gov.nb.ca/cnb/news/pre/index.htm?33,47

Speeches
http://www.gov.nb.ca/po/speech/speech.htm?41,31

LEGISLATIVE ASSEMBLY
http://www.gov.nb.ca/legis/index.htm

Speech from the Throne
http://www.gov.nb.ca/legis/busi/throne96.htm

Members
http://www.gov.nb.ca/bios/cabinet.htm

GOVERNMENT DEPARTMENTS AND AGENCIES
http://www.gov.nb.ca/dept.htm

INFORMATION HIGHWAY SECRETARIAT
http://www.gov.nb.ca/edt/infohigh/index.htm

NEW BRUNSWICK INVESTMENT OPPORTUNITIES
http://www.cybersmith.net/econ-dev/

TOURISM
http://www.gov.nb.ca/tourism/index.htm

GOVERNMENT SEARCH ENGINE
http://www.gov.nb.ca/cgibin/wwwwais

GOVERNMENT CONTACTS
http://www.gov.nb.ca/contacts/index.htm

ELECTRONIC TELEPHONE DIRECTORY
http://www.gov.nb.ca/phone/WebPH.htm

SEND YOUR COMMENTS
Email: darrelb@gov.nb.ca

Newfoundland and Labrador

http://www.gov.nf.ca/

WHAT'S NEW
http://www.gov.nf.ca/whatnew1.htm

PRESS RELEASES
http://www.gov.nf.ca/newsrel.htm

MESSAGE FROM PREMIER BRIAN TOBIN
http://www.gov.nf.ca/exec/premier/premier.htm

LEGISLATURE
http://www.gov.nf.ca/house/hoa_new.htm

MEMBERS
http://www.gov.nf.ca/house/mha.htm

CABINET
http://www.gov.nf.ca/house/cabinet.htm

1996 ELECTION RESULTS
http://www.gov.nf.ca/elect/addition.htm

BUDGET
http://www.gov.nf.ca/budget96/budget96.htm

GOVERNMENT DEPARTMENTS
http://www.gov.nf.ca/deptlst.htm

GOVERNMENT AGENCIES
http://www.gov.nf.ca/aglst.htm

ELECTRONIC TELEPHONE DIRECTORY
http://www.gov.nf.ca/wst/govphone/phtoc.html

NEWFOUNDLAND'S BUSINESS EDGE
http://www.compusult.nf.ca/ditt/edge.htm

BUSINESS OPPORTUNITIES
http://www.gov.nf.ca/itt/business/business.html

TOURISM
http://www.gov.nf.ca/itt/business/tourism.htm

View Videos
http://www.gov.nf.ca/itt/business/touravi.htm

Cabot 500 Celebrations (1997)
http://enterprise.newcomm.net/CABOT500/

HOTLIST
http://www.gov.nf.ca/sites.htm

SEND YOUR COMMENTS
Email: info@gov.nf.ca

The Northwest Territories

http://www.ssimicro.com/~xpsognwt/

PREMIER DON MORIN'S MESSAGE
http://www.ssimicro.com/~xpsognwt/Net/messages/message.html

SPEECHES AND PRESS RELEASES
http://www.ssimicro.com/~xpsognwt/Net/pr95/press.html

LEGISLATIVE ASSEMBLY
http://www.ssimicro.com/~xpsognwt/Net/assembly/Gov.html

MEMBERS
http://www.ssimicro.com/~xpsognwt/Net/assembly/mla.html

ELECTORAL MAP
http://www.ssimicro.com/~xpsognwt/Net/assembly/Election95/EDMAP
NWT.html

HISTORICAL NOTES
http://www.ssimicro.com/~xpsognwt/Net/assembly/govleaders.html

HANSARD HIGHLIGHTS
http://www.ssimicro.com/~xpsognwt/Net/pr95/statements/psa.html

GOVERNMENT PRIORITIES
http://www.ssimicro.com/~xpsognwt/Net/economy/visions.html

BUDGETARY INFORMATION
http://www.ssimicro.com/~xpsognwt/Net/economy/budget.html

LAND CLAIMS
http://www.ssimicro.com/~xpsognwt/Net/claims.html

ABORIGINAL LAW
http://fox.nstn.ca/~nstn1439/abolaw.html#top

MAJOR ISSUES
http://www.ssimicro.com/~xpsognwt/Net/issues/issues.html

DEPARTMENTS, BOARDS, AND AGENCIES
http://www.ssimicro.com/~xpsognwt/Net/departments/depart.html

ELECTRONIC TELEPHONE DIRECTORY
http://www.ssimicro.com/~xpsognwt/Net/phone/phone.html

A PICTORIAL GUIDE
http://www.ssimicro.com/~xpsognwt/Net/gallery/images.html

ARCTIC WEATHER REPORTS ·
http://www.ssimicro.com/~xpsognwt/Net/climate.html

DEMOGRAPHICS
http://www.stats.gov.nt.ca/

HOTLIST
http://www.ssimicro.com/~xpsognwt/Net/govdir.html

SEND YOUR COMMENTS
http://www.ssimicro.com/~xpsognwt/Net/messages/comments.html

Nova Scotia

http://www.gov.ns.ca/

WHAT'S NEW
http://www.gov.ns.ca/new.htm

PRESS RELEASES
http://www.gov.ns.ca/ssvs/comm/nws-rlse.htm

PREMIER JOHN SAVAGE'S WELCOME MESSAGE
http://www.gov.ns.ca/govt/welcome.htm

OFFICE OF THE PREMIER
http://www.gov.ns.ca/legi/offiprem.htm

MEMBERS OF CABINET
http://www.gov.ns.ca/legi/execcoun.htm

LEGISLATURE
http://www.gov.ns.ca/legi/

About the House of Assembly
http://www.gov.ns.ca/legi/house.htm

Directory
http://www.gov.ns.ca/legi/ha_index.htm

Members
http://www.gov.ns.ca/legi/mbrslegi.htm

Hansard
http://www.gov.ns.ca/legi/hansard.htm

GOVERNMENT DEPARTMENTS AND AGENCIES
http://www.gov.ns.ca/govt/dep-agcy.htm

ABOUT NOVA SCOTIA
http://www.gov.ns.ca/about.htm

MAP
http://www.nsgc.gov.ns.ca/samples.htm

ECONOMY AND BUSINESS
http://www.gov.ns.ca/econ-bus.htm

EDUCATION
http://www.gov.ns.ca/educ.htm

SCIENCE AND NATURE
http://www.gov.ns.ca/sci-nat.htm

TOURISM
http://www.gov.ns.ca/tourism.htm

SEARCH ENGINE
http://www.gov.ns.ca/cgi-bin/search.cmd/general

HOTLIST
http://www.gov.ns.ca/govt/links.htm

Ontario

http://www.gov.on.ca/

WHAT'S NEW
http://www.gov.on.ca/MBS/english/new/index.html

ABOUT ONTARIO
http://www.gov.on.ca/MBS/english/its_ontario/index.html

PREMIER MIKE HARRIS
http://www.gov.on.ca/MBS/english/premier/index.html

OFFICE OF THE PREMIER
http://www.gov.on.ca/MBS/english/premier/coat.html

Press Releases
gopher://govonca.gov.on.ca:70/11/po/press

Speeches and Statements
gopher://govonca.gov.on.ca:70/11/po/speech

Send Your Comments to the Premier
http://www.gov.on.ca/MBS/english/premier/reply.html

SPEECH FROM THE THRONE
http://www.gov.on.ca/MBS/english/premier/throne.html

CABINET
http://www.gov.on.ca/MBS/english/mpp/minister.html

MEMBERS OF THE LEGISLATURE
http://www.gov.on.ca/MBS/english/mpp/leg.html

BUDGET
http://www.gov.on.ca/FIN/budeng.html

CONSTITUENCY ADDRESSES
http://www.gov.on.ca/MBS/english/mpp/constit.html

GOVERNMENT DEPARTMENTS AND AGENCIES
http://www.gov.on.ca/MBS/english/government/index.html

ONTARIO ARTS COUNCIL
http://www.ffa.ucalgary.ca/oac/index.html

ONTARIO PROVINCIAL POLICE
http://www.gov.on.ca/opp/

TVONTARIO (TVO)
http://www.tvo.org/

SEND YOUR COMMENTS
http://www.gov.on.ca/MBS/english/common/feedback.html

Prince Edward Island

http://www.gov.pe.ca/

WHAT'S NEW
http://www.gov.pe.ca/new.html

LIEUTENANT GOVERNOR GILBERT CLEMENS
http://www.gov.pe.ca/lg/index.html

SPEECH FROM THE THRONE
http://www.gov.pe.ca/leg/speech.html

PREMIER CATHERINE CALLBECK
http://www.gov.pe.ca/leg/ccallbec.html

PREMIER'S GREETING
http://www.gov.pe.ca/premier/welcome.html

OFFICE OF THE PREMIER
http://www.gov.pe.ca/premier/index.html

EXECUTIVE COUNCIL (CABINET)
http://www.gov.pe.ca/ec/index.html

LEGISLATIVE ASSEMBLY
http://www.gov.pe.ca/leg/index.html

Journals
http://www.gov.pe.ca/leg/journal.html

Daily Index
http://www.gov.pe.ca/leg/bydate.html

Leader of the Official Opposition
http://www.gov.pe.ca/leg/offopp.html

Members
http://www.gov.pe.ca/leg/members.html

GOVERNMENT SERVICES
By Department
http://www.gov.pe.ca/govinfo/bydept.html

By Topic
http://www.gov.pe.ca/govinfo/bytopic.html

BUDGET
http://www.gov.pe.ca/leg/budget.html

SEARCH ENGINE
http://www.gov.pe.ca/gov-cgi-bin/gov.searchfrom.pl

BUSINESS
http://www.gov.pe.ca/picture/index.html

VISITOR'S GUIDE
http://www.gov.pe.ca/vg/index.html

THE ISLAND CAM
http://www.gov.pe.ca/islandcam/index.html

ELECTRONIC TELEPHONE DIRECTORY
http://www.gov.pe.ca/phone.html

SEND YOUR COMMENTS
http://www.gov.pe.ca/gov-cgi-bin/gov.feedback.pl

Quebec

http://www.gouv.qc.ca/

WHAT'S NEW

http://www.gouv.qc.ca/anglais/htmlsite/site_qdnf.html

PREMIER LUCIEN BOUCHARD

http://www.gouv.qc.ca/anglais/premin/premin_bio.html

Greeting

http://www.gouv.qc.ca/anglais/premin/premin_intro.html

Speeches

http://www.gouv.qc.ca/anglais/premin/premin_disc.html

Press Releases

http://www.gouv.qc.ca/anglais/premin/premin_cpress.html

Send Your Comments to the Premier

http://www.gouv.qc.ca/anglais/premin/premin_mail.html

CABINET

http://www.droit.umontreal.ca/assnat/eng/Assemblee/Fonctionnement/Personnages/titulaires.html

NATIONAL ASSEMBLY

http://www.gouv.qc.ca/anglais/assnat/an_intro.html

About the National Assembly

http://www.gouv.qc.ca/anglais/assnat/an_intro.html

Members

http://www.gouv.qc.ca/anglais/assnat/an_intro.html

GOVERNMENT DEPARTMENTS, SECRETARIATS, AND AGENCIES
http://www.gouv.qc.ca/anglais/minorg/minorg_intro.html

TOURISM AND CULTURE
http://www.gouv.qc.ca/anglais/tourcult_e/tc_intro_e.html

QUEBEC SOCIETY
http://www.gouv.qc.ca/anglais/socq/socq_intro.html

QUEBEC IN THE WORLD
http://www.gouv.qc.ca/anglais/qmond/qmond_intro.html

SEND YOUR COMMENTS
http://www.gouv.qc.ca/anglais/htmlsite/site_comments.html

Saskatchewan

http://www.gov.sk.ca/

WHAT'S NEW
http://www.gov.sk.ca/new.htm

PRESS RELEASES
http://www.sasknet.sk.ca/saskgov/govnr.html

EXECUTIVE COUNCIL
http://www.gov.sk.ca/govt/execcoun/

BUDGET
http://www.gov.sk.ca/finance/budget/budget96/96papers.htm

GOVERNMENT DEPARTMENTS
http://www.gov.sk.ca/depts.htm

GOVERNMENT AGENCIES, BOARDS, AND COMMISSIONS
http://www.gov.sk.ca/abcs.htm

CROWN CORPORATIONS
http://www.gov.sk.ca/crowns.htm

PROVINCIAL INSTITUTIONS
http://www.gov.sk.ca/institut.htm

GOVERNMENT PHONE BOOK
http://www.gov.sk.ca/spmc/phone/phone.htm

SEND YOUR COMMENTS
Email: webmaster@www.lib.sk.ca

The Yukon Territory

http://canada.gc.ca/canadiana/faitc/proyu_e.html

This site is provided by the Government of Canada and provides general, but limited, information about the Yukon and its land, history, people, and economy.

For more information about the Yukon, this second site is also worth visiting: http://www.tourYukon.com/

First Nations

Among the most active people on the Internet are the First Nations in North America. Here is a fascinating collection of links to dozens of related websites about the Cree, Innu, Mohawk Nation Council of Chiefs, Nisga'a Nation, Nunavut Implementation Commission, Chief Arthur M. Manuel's homepage from the Shuswap Nation, Akwesasne Notes magazine, Dene Cultural Institute, Nunatsiaq News, and more.

FIRST NATIONS OF THE WORLD
http://www.first-nations.com

NVWHTOHIYADA . . .

FIRST NATIONS/FIRST PEOPLE ISSUES
http://www.pobox.com/~jsd/firstnations.html
http://www.pobox.com/~jsd

CANADIAN FIRST NATIONS
http://indy4.fdl.cc.mn.us/~isk/canada/canada.htm

GREAT LAKES REGIONAL AMERICAN INDIAN NETWORK
http://www.glrain.net/glrain/

INNU NATION
http://www.web.apc.org/~innu

MOHAWK NATION COUNCIL OF CHIEFS
http://www.slic.com/~mohawk/mohawkna.htm

MOHAWK HOMEPAGE
http://www-vms.oit.umass.edu/~kahonwes/mohawk.html

AKWESASNE MOHAWK INFORMATION
http://www.slic.com/~mohawk

NISGA'A NATION
http://newswire.flexnet.com/nisgaa/#TOP

NORTHERN CREE
http://www.lib.uconn.edu/ArcticCircle/CulturalViability/Cree

NUNAVUT IMPLEMENTATION COMMISSION HOMEPAGE
http://www.nunanet.com/~nic/

SHUSWAP NATION
http://www.wp.com/Shuswap

DENE CULTURAL INSTITUTE
gopher://acs6.acs.ucalgary.ca:70/11/library/polar/institutes/dene

INTER-TRIBAL TECHNOLOGY NETWORK
http://www.phoenix.net/~ittn

LEONARD PELTIER DEFENSE COMMITTEE
http://www.unicom.net/peltier/index.html

NATIVE AMERICAN JOURNALISTS ASSOCIATION
http://www.medill.nwu.edu/naja

NATIVE BOOK CENTER
http://www.9to5.com/9to5/NBC/

NATIVE PEOPLES MAGAZINE
http://www.atiin.com/native_peoples

THE NUNATSIAQ NEWS
(Iqualuit)
http://www.nunanet.com/~nunat

ABORIGINAL EDUCATION
http://www.educ.gov.bc.ca/.abed/www/abedhome.html

NATIVE STUDIES RESOURCES IN SASKATCHEWAN
http://www.usask.ca/~siteman/sasklink.html

FOURTH WORLD DOCUMENTATION PROJECT
http://www.halcyon.com/FWDP/fwdp.html

NATIVE YOUTH WRITING PROGRAM HOMEPAGE
http://connectus.com/nywp

ABORIGINAL PEOPLES AROUND THE WORLD
http://www.io.org/~jgcom/aborl.htm

ABORIGINAL WEB LINKS IN CANADA
http://www.cyberspc.mb.ca/~fullmoon/aborig.html

ABORIGINAL YOUTH NETWORK
http://ayn-0.ayn.ca/default.htm

NATIVE BUSINESS NETWORK
http://www.capitalnet.com/~native

PEOPLE OF THE ARCTIC CIRCLE
http://www.lib.uconn.edu/ArcticCircle

NATIVE LITERATURE
http://www.indians.org/natlit.htm

FIRST NATIONS MUSIC
http://www.achilles.net/~jmerriam/first_in.html

INTERTRIBAL ART GALLERY
http://www.indart.com/gallery/gallery.htm

NATIVENET
http://www.fdl.cc.mn.us/natnet/

Intergovernmental Online

INTERGOVERNMENTAL ONLINE INFORMATION KIOSK

http://www.intergov.gc.ca

The Canadian intergovernmental online Information Kiosk is the definitive link between federal, provincial, territorial, and municipal online government activities in Canada. It also offers direct links to government resources around the world.

Visitors to this site may also wish to visit the site's documents library and join the debate at its unique virtual conference centre.

Municipal Governments

Government Online in Canada

Municipal Governments Online

Municipal government is in many ways the government that is closest to the people of any given community. The decisions that your local government makes and the activities that it undertakes can affect the safety of your streets, the quality of your drinking water, the issuance of marriage licences, the snow clearing and repairing of your roads and sidewalks, and much more.

Municipal governments in Canada are increasingly taking to the Internet to provide information and services to their residents and taxpayers. This chapter takes you directly to dozens of official and unofficial municipal sites from coast to coast to coast. More are coming online each and every day, and their cyberspace presentations are becoming increasingly impressive, informative, and intimate. Has your municipal government gone online yet?

Selected Municipalities

AMHERST, N.S.
http://rs6000.nshpl.library.ns.ca/regionals/cur/atrium.html

ANTIGONISH, N.S.
gopher://gopher.stfx.ca/11/antigonish

BANFF, ALTA.
http://www.cuug.ab.ca:8001/VT/banff-town.html

BARRIE, ONT.
http://www.city.barrie.on.ca/

BEDFORD, N.S.
http://www.cfn.cs.dal.ca/Government/Bedford/BedfordHome.html

BELLEVILLE, ONT.
http://www.telos.ca/quinte/belleville/

BIRTLE, MAN.
http://www.docker.com/~birtle/birtle.htm

BOIESTOWN, N.B.
http://www.cygnus.nb.ca/travel/boiseton.html

BRACEBRIDGE, ONT.
http://www.muskoka.com/brace.html

BRAMPTON, ONT.
http://www.city.brampton.on.ca

BRANDON, MAN.
http://www.brandonu.ca/brandon/

BROCKVILLE, ONT.
http://www.kosone.com/brockville/bwelcome.htm

BURLINGTON, ONT.
http://wchat.on.ca/cob/

CALGARY, ALTA.
http://www.gov.calgary.ab.ca/

CAMPOBELLO, N.B.
http://cnet.unb.ca/coth/nb/pages/campobello/

CANMORE, ALTA.
http://www.worldweb.com/Discover/Canmore

CAPE BRETON, N.S.
http://199.126.10.1/cbnet/govtinfo/municipa/regmenu.html

CENTRAL PLAINS, MAN.
http://www.cpnet.net/cp

CHARLOTTETOWN, P.E.I.
http://www.peinet.pe.ca/homepage/city.html

CHESTER, N.S.
http://www.isisnet.com/ChesterBound/

CHILLIWACK, B.C.
http://www.gov.chilliwack.bc.ca/

COBOURG, ONT.
http://www.eagle.ca/cobourg/

CORNWALL, ONT.
http://www.city.cornwall.on.ca/

CRANBROOK, B.C.
http://www.cyberlink.bc.ca/~pthiessen/cranb1.htm

CUMBERLAND, ONT.
http://www.municipality.cumberland.on.ca/

DARTMOUTH, N.S.
http://www.cfn.cs.dal.ca/Government/Dartmouth/DartmouthHome.html

DAWSON, YUKON
http://www.parallel.ca/yukon/YUKON-11.HTM

DEEP RIVER, ONT.
http://intranet.on.ca/deepriver/DEEP.html

EDMONTON, ALTA.
http://www.tym.com/

ELGIN AND ST-THOMAS, ONT.
http://ein.ccia.st-thomas.on.ca/~eta

ESQUIMALT, B.C.
http://www.islandnet.com/~parksrec/home.htm

ESTERHAZY, SASK.
http://www.sasknet.com/community/esterhazy

ETOBICOKE, ONT.
http://www.asgo.net/~psychic/etobicoke/etobicoke.html

FERGUS, ONT.
http://www.sentex.net/Fergus.scot/

FORTUNE, NFLD.
http://www.stemnet.nf.ca/~dreid/fortune.html

FREDERICTON, N.B.
http://degaulle.hil.unb.ca/NB/fredericton.html

GATINEAU, QUE.
http://204.19.40.10/clients/gatineau/

GLOUCESTER, ONT.
http://www.city.gloucester.on.ca/

GRANDE PRAIRIE, ALTA.
http://www.ccinet.ab.ca/city-of-gp/homepage.html

GRAVENHURST, ONT.
http://www.muskoka.com/gravenhurst

HALIFAX, N.S.
http://www.ccn.cs.dal.ca/Government/HRM/HRMHome.html

HALTON HILLS, ONT.
http://www.hhpl.on.ca/govt/hh/hh.htm

HANTS COUNTY, N.S.
http://fox.nstn.ca/~hantsrda/

HINTON, ALTA.
http://www.ycs.ab.ca/market/hinton/index.htm

HUNTSVILLE, ONT.
http://www.muskoka.com/huntsville/

KINCARDINE, ONT.
http://www.primeline.net/kincardine/kin.html

KINGSTON, ONT.
http://www.kosone.com/kaedc/Welcome.html

KIRKLAND LAKE, ONT.
http://www.northernc.on.ca/net-11/edkirk/index.htm

KITCHENER, ONT.
http://www.oceta.on.ca/city.kitchener/

LETHBRIDGE, ALTA.
http://www.city.lethbridge.ab.ca/

LINDSAY, ONT.
http://www.ptbo.igs.net/~probson/lindsay.htm

LONDON, ONT.
http://www.city.london.on.ca/

LUNENBURG, N.S.
http://www.isisnet.com/life/lunenburg/

MADAWASKA-VICTORIA, ONT.
http://www.cuslm.ca/madvic/emada-vi.htm

MERRICKVILLE, ONT.
http://www.carleton.ca/~rgray/Merrickville.html

MISSISSAUGA, ONT.
http://www.city.mississauga.on.ca/insite/html/comiss.htm

MONCTON, N.B.
http://www.umoncton.ca/regist/tourism.html

MONTREAL URBAN COMMUNITY, QUE.
http://www.cum.qc.ca/

MONT-TREMBLANT, QUE.
http://www.cam.org/~sailor/tremb1.htm

NANAIMO, B.C.
http://www.city.nanaimo.bc.ca/welcome.html

NEEPAWA, MAN.
http://www.techplus.com/neep.htm

NEPEAN, ONT.
http://www.episet.com/nepean

NEW WESTMINSTER, B.C.
http://www.pacnet.ca/newwest/

REGIONAL MUNICIPALITY OF NIAGARA, ONT.
http://vaxxine.com/region

NIAGARA FALLS, ONT.
http://www.niagara.com/city.niagara-falls/

NIPAWIN, SASK.
http://www.sasknet.com/community/Nipawin/

NORTH BAY, ONT.
http://www.city.north-bay.on.ca/northbay.htm

OAKVILLE, ONT.
http://www.town.oakville.on.ca

ORILLIA, ONT.
http://www.oyston.com/orillia/orillia.html

OTTAWA, ONT.
http://www.ncf.carleton.ca/freeport/government/ottawa/menu

OTTAWA-CARLETON REGION, ONT.
http://www.ocri.ca/rmoc/rmoc.html

PETERBOROUGH AND THE KAWARTHAS, ONT.
http://knet.flemingc.on.ca/Peterborough.html

PICTOU, N.S.
http://mfusion.com/kellock/pictou.htm

POWELL RIVER, B.C.
http://www.coc.powell-river.bc.ca/

PRINCE ALBERT, SASK.
http://www.sasknet.com/%7ecitynews/index.htm

PRINCE GEORGE, B.C.
http://vortex.netbistro.com/pg/index.html

QUEBEC CITY, QUE.
http://www.megatoon.com/web-quebec/villeqc/ville.html

RED DEER, ALTA.
http://city.red-deer.ab.ca/

ST. BRUNO-DE-MONTARVILLE, QUE.
http://www.sapience.ca/stbruno/home.htm

ST. JOHN'S, NFLD.
http://www.compusult.nf.ca/nfld/tourism/stjohns/stjohns.html

SARNIA, ONT.
http://www.sarnia.com/sarnia

SASKATOON, SASK.
http://duke.usask.ca/~lowey/Saskatoon/index.html

SAULT STE. MARIE, ONT.
http://www.soonet.ca/edc/edclgmnu.htm

SCARBOROUGH, ONT.
http://www.city.scarborough.on.ca

SHERBROOKE, QUE.
http://ville.sherbrooke.qc.ca

STRATFORD, ONT.
http://www.sentex.net/~lwr/strat.html

SUMMERSIDE, P.E.I.
http://business.atcon.com/summerside/

SYDNEY, N.S.
http://www.chatsubo.com/ecma/about_sydney.html

THUNDER BAY, ONT.
http://www.gov.on.ca/MBS/english/its_ontario/cit/thu.html

TIMMINS, ONT.
http://timmins.com/

TISDALE, SASK.
http://www.sasknet.com/community/Tisdale/

TORONTO, ONT.
http://www.toronto.com

METRO TORONTO, ONT.
http://www.metrotor.on.ca/

VANCOUVER, B.C.
http://www.city.vancouver.bc.ca/

VAUGHAN, ONT.
http://www.city.vaughan.on.ca/

VERNON, B.C.
http://www.nocdc.bc.ca/vernon/

VICTORIA, B.C.
http://www.tbc.gov.bc.ca/tourism/Victoria/victoria.html

WELLAND, ONT.
http://falls.net/nstar/weindex.htm

WHISTLER, B.C.
http://www.whistler.net/

WHITEHORSE, YUKON
http://www.tourYukon.com/YUKON-12.HTM

WINNIPEG, MAN.
http://www.freenet.mb.ca/

WOLFVILLE, N.S.
http://www.acadiau.ca/wolfville/about.html

WYNYARD, SASK.
http://www.sasknet.com/community/Wynyard/

International Relations Online

Government Online in Canada

Diplomatic Missions

Diplomacy on the Net? Of course! These links are all you need to gain direct access to Canadian diplomatic initiatives around the world and international diplomatic representatives operating in Canada.

Canada Abroad is just that: three key links that bring you directly to our embassies, missions, and honorary consuls abroad. You will find names, locations, and information to help you reach Canada's outposts around the globe.

And what of foreign countries in Canada? You will find two central weblinks with official and unofficial information about each and every country actively recognized and registered with Canadian authorities. Every foreign government embassy, high commission, and diplomatic mission operating in Canada can be traced from these URLs.

CANADA ABROAD

Our Embassies and Contact Lists
http://www.dfait-maeci.gc.ca/english/missions/

Canadian Missions Abroad
http://www.dfait-maeci.gc.ca/english/html/60/60001.htm

Honorary Consuls Abroad
http://www.dfait-maeci.gc.ca/english/html/05/05112.htm

OTHER COUNTRIES IN CANADA

Internet Directory of Diplomatic Representatives in Canada
http://www.ARRAYdev.com/commerce/emb-bck.htm

Embassies Ottawa
http://www.DocuWeb.ca/EmbassiesOttawa/

Foreign Governments

With its global reach, the Internet is helping to make the world a smaller, more accessible, and better understood place. Governments on all continents are rushing to provide online services, and in this section you will find two comprehensive lists of foreign government websites.

The first offers direct links to official government homepages — from Australia to Latvia to Peru to Saudi Arabia to Turkey to the United States.

The second list offers access to a great number of official and unofficial websites by country. In most cases they offer direct access to various foreign government departments and initiatives, and all provide important and useful information from countries like Argentina, Greece, Rwanda, and Vietnam.

OFFICIAL GOVERNMENT SITES

United Nations
http://www.un.org/

European Commission
http://www.cec.lu/

European Parliament
http://www2.echo.lu/

European Union Internet Resources
http://www.lib.berkeley.edu/GSSI/eu.html

NATO Homepage
http://www.nato.int/

International Criminal Tribunal
(Former Yugoslavia)
http://www.cij.org/tribunal/

World Bank
http://www.worldbank.org/

Agence de Cooperation Culturelle et Technique
http://www.francophonie.org

Australia
http://www.aph.gov.au/

Belgium
http://www.online.be/belgium/

Bulgaria
http://www.privatization.bg/

Chile
gopher://daniel.conicyt.cl/

China
http://www.ihep.ac.cn/china.html

Croatia
http://www.sabor.hr/

Czech Republic
gopher://fenrir.psp.cz/

Denmark
http://www.SDN.DK/

Estonia
http://www.vm.ee/

Finland
http://www.vn.fi/

France
http://www.france.diplomatie.fr/
http://www.ensmp.fr/~scherer/adminet/parliament.html
http://www.assemblee-nat.fr/ASNAT.29154.WELCOME.0.3

Georgia
http://www.parliament.ge/

Germany
http://www.bundesregierung.de/

Hong Kong
http://www.info.gov.hk

Hungarian National Assembly
http://www.mkogy.hu/

Iceland
http://www.althingi.is/

Ireland
http://www.irlgov.ie

Israel
http://www.israel-mfa.gov.il/gov/

Italy
http://www.aipa.it/
http://www.mi.cnr.it/WOI/deagosti/constitu/welcome.html

Japan
http://www.kantei.go.jp/

Kuwait
http://www.moc.kw

Latvian Saeima
http://www.saeima.lanet.lv/

Lithuania
http://rc.lrs.lt/

Luxembourg
http://www.restena.lu/luxembourg/lux_welcome.html

Malaysia
http://www.jaring.my/msia/govt/govt.html

Netherlands
http://www.dds.nl/overheid/pdc/parlement.html

New Zealand
http://www.govt.nz/
http://www.poli.govt.nz/
http://www.gwr.govt.nz

Norway
http://odin.dep.no/smk/
http://sauce.uio.no/Stortinget/English.html

Peru
http://www.rcp.net.pe/rcp/rcp-gob.html

Poland
http://www.sejm.gov.pl/

Portugal
http://infocid.sma.pt

Romania
http://diasan.vsat.ro

Russian Constitution
http://solar.rtd.utk.edu/oldfriends/constitution/russian-constitution.html

Saudi Arabia
http://imedl.saudi.net/gov_profile/consult.html

Singapore
http://www.gov.sg/

Slovakia
http://www.eunet.sk/slovakia/polit.html

Slovenia
http://www.sigov.si/dz/edz-ds.html

South Africa
http://www.polity.org.za/gnu/

ANC
http://www.polity.org.za/

Spain
http://www.la-moncloa.es/

Sweden
http://www.sb.gov.se/

Switzerland
http://www.admin.ch/

Tibet
http://www.tibet.com

Turkey
http://www.mfa.gov.tr/

Udmurtia
http://www.udm.ru

Ukraine
http://www.rada.kiev.ua/

United Kingdom
http://www.open.gov.uk/

Northern Ireland Government
http://www.nics.gov.uk/

Scottish Office
http://www.open.gov.uk/scotoff/scofhom.htm

Welsh Office
http://www.open.gov.uk/woffice/whome.htm

United States
http://www.whitehouse.gov

President Bill Clinton
Email: president@whitehouse.gov

Vice-President Al Gore
Email: vice-president@whitehouse.gov

Cap Web
http://policy.net/capweb/

American States
http://162.114.210.6/nasire/STgovernor.html

Immigration Resources
http://www.wave.net/upg/immigration/resource.html

Patent and Trademark Office
http://www.uspto.gov/

Supreme Court Decisions
http://www.law.cornell.edu/supct/

Historical Documents Archive
http://w3.one.net/~mweiler/ushda/ushda.htm

National Archives
http://www.nara.gov

U.S. Embassies and Consulates
http://www.immigration.com/us_consulates.html
http://www.globescope.com/web/gsis/embpage.html

Democratic Party
http://www.democraticparty.com

Republican Party
http://www.republicanparty.com

Glossary of U.S. Election Terms
http://www.usia.gov/elections/glossary.htm

UNOFFICIAL GOVERNMENT SITES

Afghanistan
http://frankenstein.worldweb.net/afghan

Albania
http://reenic.utexas.edu/reenic/Countries/Albania/albania.html

Antarctica
http://www.unm.edu/~vuksan/mario/news002.html

Antigua and Barbuda
http://www.interlog.com/~observer/antigua/antigua3

Arab.net
http://www.arab.net/

Argentina
http://www.yahoo.com:80/Regional/Countries/Argentina/Government/

Asia Data Disk
http://TIM.pacificnet.com/Client/HK/AsiaStudies/as.htm

Asia Pages
http://www.asiapages.com.sg

Austria
http://www.tu-graz.ac.at/1807CEAB/CInfo-AT.BM

Bahamas
http://www.travelfile.com/get?bto

Barbados
http://www.travelfile.com/get?brbds

Bermuda
http://www.travelfile.com/get?brmda

BosniaLINK
http://www.dtic.dla.mil/bosnia/

Cayman Islands
http://www.travelfile.com/get?cymnis

Colombia
http://ee1.bradley.edu/~mrr2ro/colombia/Colombia.html

Costa Rica
http://www.centralamerica.com/cr/topmenu.htm

Cubaweb
http://www.cubaweb.cu/

Curacao
http://www.travelfile.com/get?crcoto

Cyprus
http://www.geocities.com/thetropics/1093/

Egypt
http://www.channel1.com/users/mansoorm/index.html

France: The Tocqueville Connection
http://www.AdeTocqueville.com

Greece
http://www.vacation.forthnet.gr/

Hong Kong
http://www.internet-directory.com

Hong Kong Trade Development Council
http://www.tdc.org.hk/main/main.html

Indonesia Business Development
http://lookup.com/homepages/71346/home.htm

Israel
(Search engine)
http://www.xpert.com/search/

Israel's Yellow Pages
http://www.yellowpages.co.il

Jamaica
http://www.hway.net/xam/ja.htm

Japan Tibet Homepage
English Version
http://www.twics.com/~tsgjp/jthpe.html

Japanese Version
http://www.twics.com/~tsgjp/jthpj.html

Jordan
http://medcor.iconnect.com/jordan/

Lebanon
http://www.sparc.com/lebanon.html

Macedonia
http://ASUdesign.eas.asu.edu/places/Macedonia/republic/news/

Mexico
http://www.mexicosi.com

Palestine
http://http2.brunel.ac.uk:8080/~em93mma/

Papua New Guinea
http://coombs.anu.edu.au/SpecialProj/PNG/WWWVL-PNG.html

Rwanda
http://www.interpac.be/rwanda/

United States
http://206.74.57.36/geography/usa/page00.htm

Vietnam
http://www.cgtd.com/global/vietnam.html

Political Parties

Government Online in Canada

Political Parties Online

Canadian political parties, on both a national and a provincial level, have greatly increased their online activism in recent months. As you will see by the listing in this section, most parties across the country have established Internet outposts and are utilizing their websites as key elements of their ongoing political operations.

Visitors will find a variety of partisan information about a party's elected representatives, officers, platform, legislative initiatives, fundraising activities, and membership forms. Many sites also offer links around the globe to kindred spirits across the political spectrum.

Federal Political Parties

LIBERAL PARTY OF CANADA
http://www.liberal.ca

BLOC QUÉBÉCOIS
http://www.opposition.bloc.ca

REFORM PARTY OF CANADA
http://www.reform.ca

PROGRESSIVE CONSERVATIVE PARTY OF CANADA
http://www.pcparty.ca

NEW DEMOCRATIC PARTY OF CANADA
http://fed.ndp.ca/fndp/

LIBERTARIAN PARTY
http://clipper.uvic.ca/GVLA/

GREEN PARTY OF CANADA
http://onlinedirect.com/green/home.html

COMMUNIST PARTY OF CANADA (MARXIST-LENINIST)
http://fox.nstn.ca/~cpc-ml/index.html

CHRISTIAN HERITAGE PARTY OF CANADA
http://ourworld.compuserve.com/homepages/Jeffrey_Streutker/chp.htm

Provincial Political Parties

ALBERTA

PC
http://www.albertapc.ab.ca/

NDP
gopher://freenet.edmonton.ab.ca/11/i/newdems

Liberals
http://www.freenet.calgary.ab.ca/politics/province/ablib/

Social Credit Party
gopher://freenet.edmonton.ab.ca/hi/socred/socred.html

Alberta Green Party
http://envirolink.org/greens/canada/alberta.html

BRITISH COLUMBIA

NDP
http://www.bc.ndp.ca/

Liberals
http://vvv.com/liberals/

Progressive Democratic Alliance of B.C.
http://www.islandnet.com/~alliance/pda.html

Green Party of B.C.
http://www.alternatives.com/groups/wwwgreen/index.htm

British Columbia First Alliance Association
http://www.islandnet.com/~bcfirst/

MANITOBA
NDP
http://www.ndpcaucus.mb.ca

Liberals
http://pooh.freenet.mb.ca/BSFN/iphome/l/lib-mb/index.html

PC
http://alpha.remcan.ca/filmonteam/index.html

NEW BRUNSWICK
Liberals
http://www.staccato.nb.ca/nblib

NDP
http://www.io.org/~alexng/nd/nbwin.html

PC
http://www.pcparty.nb.ca/

NEWFOUNDLAND AND LABRADOR
Liberals
http://www.newcomm.net/liberal/default.htm

PC
http://www.compusult.nf.ca/~verge/

NOVA SCOTIA
NDP
http://cfn.cs.dal.ca/Politics/NSNewDemocrat/ndphp.html

ONTARIO
PC
http://www.ontariopc.on.ca/

NDP
http://www.ncf.carleton.ca/freeport/government/provelect/parties/ndp/menu

Green Party of Ontario
http://idirect.com/election/green.html
http://206.210.73.7/greens/ontario/

Communist Party
http://idirect.com/election/communist.html

Confederation of Regions Party
http://idirect.com/election/regents.html

Family Coalition Party
http://idirect.com/election/family.html

Freedom Party of Canada
http://idirect.com/election/freedom.html

Natural Law Party of Ontario
http://idirect.com/election/nlp/nlp.html

QUEBEC
Parti Québécois
http://www.itr.qc.ca/PQ/

Action Democratique
http://www.itr.qc.ca/ADQ_OUI_DUMONT/

YUKON TERRITORY
Yukon Party
http://www.yukonweb.wis.net/community/yukon-party/

Afterword

by Mike Duffy, Ottawa editor,
BBS News, Baton Broadcasting System

An informed public is the hallmark of a democratic society. And today the Internet, the World Wide Web, and the proliferation of other online services all mean that the opportunity for citizens to participate in their democracy has never been greater.

Alexander Graham Bell came up with the idea of "electric speech" in 1875 while visiting his parents in Brantford, Ontario. It was a brilliant idea, but a bit slow to take off. In 1945, at the end of the Second World War, fewer than half the homes in Canada had telephone service.

But if it took a while for Bell's idea to catch on, the communications explosion in the fifty years since the end of the war has more than made up for lost time. Today, not only does every home in Canada have a telephone, but there is actually one phone for every 1.3 persons living in Canada. And the experts tell us that Canadians are the most avid users of telephone services on earth.

And that usage is expanding as the Internet grows. The telephone, and its associated communications devices, the fax and the computer, can now operate from literally anywhere on the face of the globe. When that ability to communicate is linked with the vast storehouse of information available via the Internet, the result is mind-boggling.

The Government of Canada has been at the forefront of the effort to "go online" — to make its files available to its citizens. There are literally hundreds of databases, involving every area of government activity, that are now accessible via the Internet.

As with anything new, however, we need a guide to show us the way around, and to help us get the most from the Internet maze. That's where this book comes in. Pierre Bourque, a young man who traded his passion for racing cars for the calmer world of the computer geek, takes the mystery out of the Net. Here you learn the fast and easy way to the places you need and, even more fun, the fast and easy way to the *fun* spots on the Net.

Netting is important, serious work, but it is also fun. Pierre shows us all how to learn and enjoy.

See you on the Net.

Mike Duffy (sundayed@baton.com), March 1996

Appendices

Government Online in Canada

Appendix A: A History of the Internet

The Internet is growing at an astounding pace. No other communication tool and cultural phenomenon has experienced this level of progress in such a relatively short period of time. But how did it all begin? What have been its principal milestones along the way?

Get the complete history of the Net at the Hobbes' Internet Timeline. It offers the Internet's history, complete with relevant stats, facts, and charts. Best of all, it is continually updated and is full of useful hotlinks that let you explore related historical moments in the life of the Internet.

HOBBES' INTERNET TIMELINE

http://www.cob.ohio-state.edu/facstf/homepage/muhanna/pre/history.html

And make sure that you stop by the following site, which celebrates the Internet's twenty-fifth anniversary (1994):

INTERNET 25TH ANNIVERSARY

http://www.amdahl.com/internet/events/inet25.html

Finally, here is a site which brings together the full breadth of the Internet on a single day:

A DAY IN THE LIFE OF CYBERSPACE

http://www.1010.org/

Appendix B: Key Electronic Addresses

The following is a list of key email and web addresses of elected members of the Parliament of Canada, the Senate, and the provincial legislatures.

PARLIAMENT OF CANADA

Liberal Party of Canada

Reg Alcock
winnipeg_south@mbnet.mb.ca
http://www.mbnet.mb.ca/wpgsth

Lloyd Axworthy, Minister of Foreign Affairs
lloyd.axworthy@hrdc-drhc.gc.ca

Don Boudria, Chief Government Whip
boudrd@parl.gc.ca

Mary Clancy
clancm@parl.gc.ca

David Dingwall, Minister of Health
dingwd@parl.gc.ca

John English
englij@parl.gc.ca
http://tdg.uoguelph.ca/~jenglish/

Dr. Jon Gerrard
minister.science@ic.gc.ca or
Portage_Interlake@mbnet.mb.ca
http://www.freenet.mb.ca/mp/gerrardj/

Ivan Grose
igrosemp@msn.com

John Manley, Minister of Industry
manley.john@istc.ca

Paul Martin, Minister of Finance
pmartin@fin.gc.ca

Rey Pagtakhan
pagtar@parl.gc.ca

Alex Shepherd
ashepher@chat.carleton.ca

Paddy Torsney
torsnp@parl.gc.ca

Bloc Québécois

Real Menard
menarr@parl.gc.ca

Reform Party of Canada

Preston Manning, Leader
leader@reform.ca

Reform House Leader
speaker@reform.ca

Jim Abbott
abbott@reform.ca

Diane Ablonczy
ablonczy@reform.ca
http://www.reform.ca/english/mps/ablonczy/ablonczy.html

Leon Benoit
benoit@reform.ca

Cliff Breitkreuz
breitkreuzc@reform.ca

Garry Breitkreuz
breitkreuzg@reform.ca

Margaret Bridgman
bridgman@reform.ca

John Cummins
cummins@reform.ca

John Duncan
duncan@reform.ca

Ken Epp
epp@reform.ca

Paul Forseth
forseth@reform.ca

Jack Frazer
frazer@reform.ca

Bill Gilmour
gilmour@reform.ca
http://www.reform.ca/english/mps/gilmour/gilmour.html

Jim Gouk
gouk@reform.ca

Deborah Grey
grey@reform.ca

Herb Grubel
grubel@reform.ca

Art Hanger
hanger@reform.ca

Hugh Hanrahan
hanrahan@reform.ca

Ed Harper
harpere@reform.ca

Stephen Harper
harpers@reform.ca

Dick Harris
harris@reform.ca
http://www.reform.ca/english/mps/harris/harris.html

Jim Hart
hart@reform.ca

Sharon Hayes
hayes@reform.ca
http://www.reform.ca/english/mps/hayes/index.html

Elwin Hermanson
hermanson@reform.ca

Grant Hill
hillg@reform.ca

Jay Hill
hillj@reform.ca

Jake Hoeppner
hoeppner@reform.ca

Daphne Jennings
jennings@reform.ca

Dale Johnston
johnston@reform.ca

Allan Kerpan
kerpan@reform.ca

Preston Manning
pmanning@reform.ca

Keith Martin
martin@reform.ca
http://www.islandnet.com/~kmp/homepage.htm

Philip Mayfield
mayfield@reform.ca

Ian McClelland
mcclelland@reform.ca

Val Meredith
meredith@reform.ca

Bob Mills
mills@reform.ca

Lee Morrison
morrison@reform.ca

Charlie Penson
pensoc@parl.gc.ca

Jack Ramsay
ramsay@reform.ca

Bob Ringma
ringma@reform.ca

Werner Schmidt
schmidt@reform.ca
http://www.reform.ca/english/mps/schmidt/werner.html

Mike Scott
scott@reform.ca

Jim Silye
silye@reform.ca
http://www.reform.ca/english/mps/silye/silye.html

Monte Solberg
solberg@reform.ca

Ray Speaker
speaker@reform.ca

Darrel Stinson
stinson@reform.ca

Chuck Strahl
strahl@reform.ca

Myron Thompson
thompson@reform.ca

Randy White
whiter@reform.ca

Ted White
whitet@reform.ca

John Williams
williams@reform.ca

New Democratic Party
Audrey McLaughlin
mclaua@parl.gc.ca

THE SENATE
Liberal Party
Dan Hays
bd439@freenet.carleton.ca

PROVINCIAL LEGISLATURES
Alberta Legislative Assembly
Michael Henry
mhenry@ccinet.ab.ca

Premier Ralph Klein
altatalk@censsw.gov.ab.ca

British Columbia Legislative Assembly
David Schreck
davids@cyberstore.ca

Gordon Wilson
alliance@islandnet.com

Manitoba Legislative Assembly

Premier Gary Filmon
premier@leg.gov.mb.ca

New Brunswick Legislative Assembly

Edmond Blanchard
blanchard@gov.nb.ca

Ann Breault
annb@gov.nb.ca

Georges Corriveau
georgesc@gov.nb.ca

Laureen Jarrett
ljarrett@gov.nb.ca

James Lockyer
jamesl@gov.nb.ca

Allan Maher
amaher@gov.nb.ca

Leo McAdam
leom@gov.nb.ca

Premier Frank McKenna
premier@gov.nb.ca

Marcelle Mersereau
marcellm@gov.nb.ca

Brent Taylor
mla30@nbnet.nb.ca

Camille Theriault
cth@gov.nb.ca

Nova Scotia House of Assembly

Alan Mitchell
amitchel@fox.nstn.ca

Premier John Savage
jsavage@fox.nstn.ca

Ontario Provincial Parliament
Premier Mike Harris
premier@gov.on.ca

Quebec National Assembly
Premier Lucien Bouchard
premier.ministre@gouv.qc.ca

Equality Party
egalite@CAM.ORG

Saskatchewan Legislative Assembly
Progressive Conservative Caucus
pccaucus@microcity.com

Appendix C: Glossaries of Terms

New technology demands new language. Here are several extremely useful online glossaries that benefit from continuous updating.

PUBLIC WORKS CANADA (PWC) TERMINOLOGY LINKS
http://w3.pwgsc.gc.ca/text/terms-e.html

MANAGEMENT AND TECHNOLOGY DICTIONARY
http://www.euro.net/innovation/Management_Base/Mantec.Dictionary.html

NETGLOS
(A multilingual glossary of Internet terms)
http://wwli.com/translation/netglos/netglos.html

BABEL
(A glossary of computer-oriented abbreviations and acronyms)
http://www.access.digex.net/~ikind/babel96b.html

THE MATISSE GLOSSARY OF TERMS, BY THE INTERNET LITERACY CONSULTANTS
http://www.matisse.net/files/glossary.html

EUROVOC THESAURUS
gopher://fenrir.psp.cz:70/11/eurovoc/english

Appendix D: Online Resources

Here is your guide to the online motherlode of Internet treasures: links to important Internet-related associations and activists; key business organizations; computer hardware, software, and wetware manufacturers and developers; important documents that guide the principles of our democracy's rights and freedoms; educational tools like the *World Lecture Hall*, *Old Farmer's Almanac*, foreign-language translators, dictionaries, and *Bartlett's Book of Familiar Quotations*; and much more — like NASA's homepage, a Reporter's Internet Survival Guide, and a great many links to free software and the latest online technology resources, to help you understand, access, and enjoy every facet of the Internet.

ASSOCIATIONS AND ACTIVISTS

CA*Net
http://www.canet.ca/canet/

Center for Democracy and Technology (U.S.)
http://www.cdt.org/

Chronicle of Freedom of Expression in Canada
http://insight.mcmaster.ca/org/efc/pages/chronicle/chronicle.html

Coalition for Public Information
gopher://gabriel.resudox.net.:1994/1

Electronic Frontier Canada
http://www.efc.ca

Electronic Frontier Foundation (U.S.)
http://www.eff.org

Electronic Privacy Information Center (EPIC)
http://www.epic.org/

Information Highway Working Group
http://kows.web.net/ihwg/

Internet Public Interest Research Group (IPIRG)
http://tdg.res.uoguelph.ca/~ipirg/

The Loka Institute (U.S.)
http://www.amherst.edu/~loka/

Network Canada Alliance
http://www.lglobal.com/connect/

Public - Information Highway Advisory Council (P-IHAC)
http://www.carleton.ca/~swyerxa/p-ihac.html

Telecommunities Canada
http://www.freenet.mb.ca/tc/index.html

BUSINESS

Canada Business Service Centre (CBSC)
http://www.dfait-maeci.gc.ca/english/html/10/10002.htm

International Trade Centres in Canada
http://www.dfait-maeci.gc.ca/english/html/60/60002.htm

Trade Offices in Ottawa
(International Business Development Divisions)
http://www.dfait-maeci.gc.ca/english/html/05/05103.htm

Securities and Exchange Commission (U.S.)
http://www.sec.gov/

Apple
http://www.info.apple.com/

Corel
http://www.corel.com

Dell
http://www.dell.com/

Digital
http://www.dec.com/

Hewlett-Packard
http://www.hp.com/

IBM
http://www.ibm.com/

Lotus Development Corp.
http://www.lotus.com/

Microsoft
http://www.microsoft.com/

Novell
http://www.novell.com/

Silicon Graphics
http://www.sgi.com/

Sun Microsystems
http://www.sun.com/

EDUCATIONAL

World Constitutions
ftp://wiretap.spies.com/Gov/World/

Education Organizations in Canada
http://www.dfait-maeci.gc.ca/english/culture/menu.htm

Index of Canadian Universities and Colleges
http://www.intergov.gc.ca/PSECSTUD/psecindx.html

Canadian Charter of Rights and Freedoms
http://insight.mcmaster.ca/org/efc/pages/law/charter/charter.head.html

Canadian Bill of Rights
http://insight.mcmaster.ca/org/efc/pages/law/canada/BillofRights.html

Criminal Code of Canada
http://insight.mcmaster.ca/org/efc/pages/law/cc/cc.html

Canadian Constitutional Documents
http://insight.mcmaster.ca/org/efc/pages/law/cons/constitutions.html

Canadian Human Rights Act
http://insight.mcmaster.ca/org/efc/pages/law/canada/canada.H-6.head.html

Canadian Human Rights Campaign
http://www.io.org/~chrc

Universal Declaration of Human Rights (U.N.)
http://insight.mcmaster.ca/org/efc/pages/law/un/un-rights.html

Research It
(Contains dictionaries, thesauruses, language translators, acronyms, quotations, maps, telephone numbers, postal information, package tracking, financial info, and more)
http://www.iTools.com/research-it/research-it.html

SchoolNet
http://schoolnet2.carleton.ca

World Lecture Hall
http://www.utexas.edu/world/lecture/index.html

Canada EarthSave
http://www.earthsave.bc.ca

WWW Virtual Library
http://www.w3.org/hypertext/DataSources/bySubject/Overview.html

Black History
http://www.gatech.edu/bgsa/blackpages.html

Martin Luther King's "I Have a Dream" Speech
http://web66.coled.umn.edu/new/MLK/MLK.html

Inventors' Hall of Fame
http://www.invent.org/book/index.html

Food and Nutrition
http://ificinfo.health.org/index.htm

Quebec Referendum (1995)
YES Side
http://quebec-oui.org

NO Side
http://www.comite-non.qc.ca

American Civil Liberties Union
http://www.aclu.org

NASA
http://www.gsfc.nasa.gov/NASA_homepage.html

U.S. Telecom Legislation
http://www.technologylaw.com/techlaw/telecom_bill.html

JOURNALISM
A Reporter's Internet Survival Guide
http://www.qns.com/~casey/

Quebec Launch Pad for Journalists
http://www.vir.com/~andymon

Yellow Pages of Quebec Enterprises
http://www.quebecweb.com/entreprises/

WWW Sources for Journalists and Broadcasters
http://www.synapse.net/~radio/welcome.html

Public Relations Agencies and Resources
http://www.webcom.com/impulse/prlist.html

Public Affairs Web (U.S.)
http://www.publicaffairsweb.com/mainmenu.htm

Private Sector Press Releases
http://www.pressline.com/homepage.html

Canadian Association of Chiefs of Police
(Resolution relating to the Internet)
http://insight.mcmaster.ca/org/efc/pages/law/doc/cacp.24aug95.html#3

Government Policy Documents About the Information Highway
(From around the world)
http://www.nla.gov.au/lis/govnii.html

Industry Canada Background Paper
(Pertaining to illegal and offensive content on the Information Highway)
http://insight.mcmaster.ca/org/efc/pages/doc/offensive.html

U.S. Telecommunications Law
http://thomas.loc.gov/home/hot-titl.html

Information Warfare and Cyberspace Security
http://www.rand.org/publications/RRR/RRR.fall95.cyber/

Guide to Internet Use in the Federal Government
http://www.tbs-sct.gc.ca/tb/pubs/in/ine.html

Links to Intelligence-Related Sites
http://www.kimsoft.com/kim-spy.htm

Central Intelligence Agency
http://www.odci.gov/cia

United States Intelligence Community
http://www.odci.gov/ic

Spy Material on the Web
http://www.kimsoft.com/kim-spy.htm

Strategic Intelligence Home Site
http://www.loyola.edu/dept/politics/intel.html

Terrorist Profile Weekly
http://www.site.gmu.edu/~cdibona/

FBI's Ten Most Wanted
http://www.fbi.gov/toplist.htm

TECHNOLOGY

CANARIE
http://www.canarie.ca/

McLuhan Program in Culture and Technology
http://www.fis.utoronto.ca/mcluhan/

ONLINE TOOLS

Beginner's Guide to HTML
http://www.ncsa.uiuc.edu/General/Internet/WWW/HTMLPrimer.html

About the Online World
http://www.vol.it/UK/EN/INFO/online23.htm

About Private Key Encryption
(Pretty good privacy — PGP)
http://www.hwc.ca/links/tech/email/pgp.htm

About Security and the Internet
http://www.hwc.ca/links/tech/security.htm

Anonymous Remailers
(Anonymous email accounts)
http://electron.rutgers.edu/~gambino/anon_servers/anon.html

Bartlett, John. 1901. Familiar Quotations
http://www.columbia.edu/acis/bartleby/bartlett/

Beginner's Guide to the Internet
http://www.yahoo.com/computers_and_internet/internet/information_and_documentation/beginner_s_guides/

Books About the Internet
http://www.northcoast.com/savetz/booklist

Build Your Own Web Page
http://www.fn.net/~bkreed/author.html

Computer Beginner's Home Page
http://www.southam.com/nmc/guide/computips/complist.html

Current Time Around the World
http://www.brunel.co.uk/davidw/_FIFTEEN.html

CyberAtlas
http://www.cyberatlas.com

Daily Almanac
http://www.eecs.uic.edu/~mmaggio/almanac2.html

Documents Related to Online Services in Canada
http://www.intergov.gc.ca/IGDOCLIP/FEDGOV/fedindxe

Download Browsers and Add-ons
(Netscape, Mosaic, Lynx, etc)
http://www.hwc.ca/links/tech/browsers.htm

Download Multilingual Browser from Video Online
(A free Internet browser for Mac and Windows 95 in 18 languages, including Arabic and Chinese)
http://www.vol.it/VOLB/browser.html

Earthquake Maps and Lists
http://www.primenet.com/~shorose/history.html

Foreign Languages for Travellers
http://www.travlang.com/languages/

Gamelan
(Loads of Java applets)
http://www.gamelan.com

GIF Converter
(For images)
http://www.kamit.com/gifconverter.html

HotJava
http://www.hotjava.com

Internet Access Providers Around the World
http://www.best.be/iap.html

Internet Browsers and Viewers
http://pilot.msu.edu/user/heinric6/tools.htm

Internet Connectivity Map
http://www.NRCan.gc.ca/Connectivity_Map.color.gif

Internet Conference Calendar
http://www.automatrix.com/conferences/

Internet Demographic Survey Results
http://www.survey.net/sv-inet1.htm

Internet Fax Server
http://sable.ox.ac.uk/fax/

Internet Multimedia
http://www.hwc.ca/links/tech/multimed/audvideo.html

Internet Shopper
(Listing of Internet-related software and hardware product suppliers)
http://www.iworld.com/InternetShopper/

Internet Statistics
http://www.openmarket.com/info/internet-index/current.html

Internet Guide in French
http://www.imaginet.fr/~gmaire/toc.htm

Internet Training Resources
http://www.brandonu.ca/~ennsnr/Resources/resources.html

InterNIC Directory
http://www.internic.net/

Liszt: Searchable Directory of Email Discussion Groups
http://www.liszt.com/

MUD and MOO Directory
http://mbhs.bergtraum.k12.ny.us/moo.html

National Weather
gopher://cmits02.dow.on.doe.ca:70/19/maps/cansysy

Netscape
http://home.netscape.com/

Network Survival Kit
(For systems administrators)
http://www.ctyme.com/nsk.htm

Old Farmer's Almanac
http://www.xensei.com/ofa/

Public Works and Government Services (PWGSC) — Internet Guides Bookmarks
http://w3.pwgsc.gc.ca/text/guides-e.html

Real Audio
http://www.realaudio.com

Reference
(A tremendous collection of tools)
http://www2.eos.net/Info4Hire/index.html

Richter Magnitude
(Size of an earthquake)
http://www.seismo.unr.edu/ftp/pub/louie/class/100/magnitude.html

Send a Fax by Email
http://www.engin.umich.edu/htbin/faxnum-check

Switchboard
(Over 90 million telephone numbers)
http://www.switchboard.com/

Web Authoring Resources
http://www.cisti.nrc.ca/cisti/webstuff.html

WebPhone
http://www.netspeak.com

Web Publishers Pages
http://w3.pwgsc.gc.ca:80/text/pblish-e.html

Windows 95
http://www.hwc.ca/links/tech/win95_e.htm

Winsock
http://mars.superlink.net/user/mook/winfaq.html

Appendix E: Selected Media Links

You will find the following collection of media links to be extremely useful for two reasons. First, because government and other political activities traditionally come under close scrutiny by the media. These addresses provide links to government and parliamentary media, newspapers, magazines, broadcasters, and news agencies from around the world. You will find among the features offered at these sites considerable political and governmental information that will increase your understanding of what's happening in Canada and abroad.

And since this book deals with government and politics as it pertains to a highly advanced technological medium, links have also been included to most of the important media operations focusing on technology.

GOVERNMENT RELATED

Hill Times
http://www.thehilltimes.ca

Technocracy
(The online magazine of government technology)
http://www.hum.com/

HUM — The Government Computer Magazine
http://www.hum.com/hum1st.html

Canadian Parliamentary Review
http://www.magi.com/~infoparl

Cable Parliamentary Channel
http://www.screen.COM/cpac

National Press Club
http://www.ottawa.net/~presclub/

TECHNOLOGY PUBLICATIONS

Computer Paper
http://www.tcp.ca/

Silicon Valley North
http://www.silvan.com/

Data Communications
http://www.data.com

Macworld Online
http://www.macworld.com/

Monitor
http://www.monitor.ca/monitor/index.html

PC Magazine
http://www.zdnet.com/pcmag/

PC Computing
http://www.zdnet.com/pccomp/

Computer Shopper
http://www.zdnet.com/cshopper/

Windows Sources
http://www.zdnet.com/wsources/

MacUser
http://www.zdnet.com/macuser/

MacWeek
http://www.zdnet.com/macweek/

Interactive Week
http://www.zdnet.com/intweek/

Computer Life
http://www.zdnet.com/complife/

Family PC
http://www.zdnet.com/familypc/

Computer Gaming World
http://www.zdnet.com/gaming/

Internet Life
http://www.zdnet.com/zdil/

Wired/HotWired
http://www.hotwired.com

NEWSPAPERS

Newspaper Chains
http://www.mediainfo.com/edpub/e-papers.newschains.html

Southam
http://www.southam.com/

Sterling Newspapers
http://www.sterlingnews.com/

Sun
http://www.canoe.ca/

International Thomson Publishing
http://www.thomson.com/

List of Canadian Newspapers Online
http://www.mediainfo.com/edpub/e-papers.canada.html

Canadian Press and Broadcast News
http://www.xe.net/canpress/

Globe and Mail
http://www.globeandmail.ca/

Halifax Daily News
http://www.cfn.cs.dal.ca/Media/TodaysNews/TodaysNews.html

Northern Miner
http://www.southam.com/northernminer/

North Shore News
(Vancouver)
http://www.nsnews.com

Ottawa Citizen
http://www.ottawacitizen.com/

Ottawa Xpress
http://www.theottawaxpress.ca/

Vancouver Echo
http://www.vannet.com/VANECHO/default.htm

Winnipeg Free Press
http://www.freepress.mb.ca/freepress

Times of London
http://www.the-times.co.uk/

Roll Call
http://www.rollcall.com

Capitol Watch On Line
http://www.capitolwatch.com

Congressional Quarterly
http://voter96.cqalert.com

New York Times
http://www.nytimes.com/

New York Times Syndicate
http://nytsyn.com

Wall Street Journal
http://update.wsj.com/

Tribune Co.
http://www.tribune.com/

USA Today
http://www.usatoday.com/

MAGAZINES

Editor & Publisher Interactive
http://www.mediainfo.com/edpub/

Time Magazine
http://www.time.com

Utne Reader
http://www.utne.com/

MISCELLANEOUS

News and Current Events
http://www.yahoo.com/News/Current_Events/

World News Index
http://toad.stack.urc.tue.nl/~haroldkl/index.html

Voice of America
gopher://gopher.voa.gov

Canada News Wire
http://www.newswire.ca/

Electronic Newsstand
http://www.enews.com/

Rogers Communication
http://www.rogers.com/

PBS
http://www.pbs.org/

CBC
http://www.cbc.ca/

CTV
http://www.cs.cmu.edu/afs/cs.cmu.edu/user/clamen/misc/tv/Canada/CTV-sched.html

ABC
http://www.abc.com

CBS
http://www.cbs.com

NBC
http://www.nbc.com

CNN AllPolitics
http://www.allpolitics.com

National Public Broadcasting Archives (U.S.)
http://www.itd.umd.edu/UMS/UMCP/NPBA/npba.html

BBC
http://www.bbc.co.uk/

Agence France Presse
http://www.afp.com/

NewsLink
(Links to every paper with online versions)
http://www.newslink.org

Web Newstand
http://www.web-newsstand.com

International Internet NewsClips
http://metday.iworld.com

Eurasia Research Center
http://ourworld.compuserve.com/homepages/EurasiaRC

Asia Pacific Economic Review
http://www.moshix2.net/APER/

Argentina Headline News
http://www.webcom.com/poetas/interlink/ilhn.html

Chinese Media Information
(China, Taiwan, Hong Kong, Singapore, and Canadian-Chinese media)
http://www.wt.net/~alex/html/media.htm

Filipinas Online
http://www.filipinas.com

India Infobase
http://www.webcom.com/~prakash

Indonesia News
http://www.newsindonesia.com

Latin American News
http://www.ozemail.com.au/~ecuapita/latam.html

Middle Eastern and African, Islamic, and Arabic Newspapers
http://erau.db.erau.edu/~al-zarom

Pakistani Newspapers Online
http://www.hgmp.mrc.ac.uk/~npanjwan/PAKnewslist.html

Philippine News Agency
http://www.mabuhay.com/Balita-L/

Russian Media on the Web
http://www.hibo.no/stud/sh4/media.html

Singapore Internet News
http://odin.pacific.net.sg/dmedia/intnews.html

Vietnow Magazine
http://www.vietnow.com/content.html

Xinhua News Agency
(People's Republic of China)
http://www.attaina.com

Appendix F: Search Engines

Search engines are marvellous tools designed to help you locate and access information on the Internet. You will find the following comprehensive list of government and public search engines to be an invaluable research assistant as you manipulate government information and mine data.

Use the government search engines to find specific government data and the others to retrieve just about anything that exists on the Net. They are truly wonderful tools, which will cut your research time drastically.

Additional search engines specific to various governments and departments are provided elsewhere in this book. Look for them when you access specific government web pages.

GOVERNMENT SEARCH ENGINES

Government of Canada Website
http://canada.gc.ca/search/srcind_e.html

Champlain: Federal, Provincial, and Municipal Sites
http://champlain.gns.ca/champlain.html

Government Information Finder Technology (GIFT)
http://canada.gc.ca/search/colind_e.html

THOMAS: Legislative Information on the Net (U.S.)
http://thomas.loc.gov/

INTERNET SEARCH ENGINES

AliWeb
http://www.cs.indiana.edu/aliweb/form.html

Alta Vista
http://www.altavista.digital.com/

Area Code Directory
http://www.555-1212.com/aclookup.html

Canadian Information
http://www.cs.cmu.edu/afs/cs.cmu.edu/user/clamen/misc/Canadiana/CA-gophers.html

Canadian WWW Index
http://WWW.CSR.ISTS.CA/w3can/Welcome.html

Computer ESP — Electronic Search Page
http://www.uvision.com/

DejaNews
(Great for sifting through Usenet)
http://dejanews.com/

Eureka!
http://www.best.com/~mentorms/eureka.htm

European Directory
http://www.ukshops.co.uk:8000/thedoor.html

Excite Netsearch
http://www.excite.com/

Find Email Addresses
http://www.four11.com/

Finger Gateway
(Find user information from an email address)
http://www-bprc.mps.ohio-state.edu/cgi-bin/finger.pl

Infoseek
(Fee based)
http://www.infoseek.com/

Internet Address Finder
http://www.iaf.net/

Inktomi
http://inktomi.berkeley.edu/

Lycos
http://query1.lycos.cs.cmu.edu/lycos-form.html

OpenText
http://www.opentext.com/

SavvySearch
http://www.cs.colostate.edu/~dreiling/smartform.html

TradeWave Galaxy
http://www.einet.net/

WebCrawler
http://webcrawler.com/

The Whois Command
(Provides details about an Internet host)
http://union.ncsa.uiuc.edu/whoispp.html

Yahoo
http://www.yahoo.com